Forgiveness

Forgiveness

A Practical and Pastoral Companion

Anthony Priddis

CANTERBURY
PRESS
Norwich

© Anthony Priddis 2019

First published in 2019 by the Canterbury Press Norwich
Editorial office
3rd Floor, Invicta House
108–114 Golden Lane
London EC1Y OTG, UK
www.canterburypress.co.uk

Canterbury Press is an imprint of Hymns Ancient & Modern Ltd
(a registered charity)

Hymns Ancient & Modern® is a registered trademark of
Hymns Ancient & Modern Ltd
13A Hellesdon Park Road, Norwich,
Norfolk NR6 5DR, UK

British Library Cataloguing in Publication data

A catalogue record for this book is available
from the British Library

978 1 78622 138 4

Typeset by Regent Typesetting
Printed and bound in Great Britain by
CPI Group (UK) Ltd

Contents

I

Why forgiveness matters

'Have you forgiven your captors yet?'

'No. Never.'

'Then it seems like they still have you in prison, don't they?'

Three ex-prisoners of war stood in front of the Vietnam Veterans Memorial in Washington DC, and this was their conversation.

It was depicted on the front cover of a winter edition of *Spirituality and Health*[1] and it focuses succinctly and sharply on why forgiveness matters so very much.

It is a conversation that we all need to hear because it applies to all situations, not just the horror of having been a prisoner of war or suffering the nightmare of torture. Not forgiving keeps us locked in prison. We need a way out and forgiveness is that way. We may think that forgiveness is primarily for the benefit of the person who has done the wrong, caused the harm, the pain and suffering, but it is also for the person offended and hurt. The one who has suffered *needs to be able to forgive*, just as the one who has caused the suffering *needs to be forgiven*. Both are vital. We offer forgiveness to one another because we need to, not just because the other person needs to receive it. If, like the soldier, we don't offer forgiveness then we stay imprisoned by our revenge and bitterness. If we don't receive forgiveness for harm we have caused and for which we are responsible then we stay imprisoned by our guilt. We want and need to be out of prison, both prisons. We need both to forgive and to be forgiven. It is essential for our own sake, not just for the sake of the other who has harmed us, or we have harmed.

Abuse and horror cause trauma, pain, anguish, anger, guilt and suffering which can continue for years, sometimes for a lifetime. In the face of all that, how can people possibly find a way out of prison and forgive?

For those who have suffered and continue to suffer, there is a way, and it is open to all of us if we really want to find it and choose to begin the journey.

Forgiveness is a costly journey because there is no such thing as 'cheap grace'[2] or cheap forgiveness or, if there is, it is not worth having, giving or receiving. Costly though it may be, the alternative is far costlier: it is far more damaging to us because it leaves us in prison. The journey begins with wanting to forgive or, if even that seems too difficult, with wanting to want to forgive. It is a process. Very few of us, if any, can jump straight to complete forgiveness when violence and extreme suffering are involved, but there are ways of making a start, of beginning the process and walking the path that takes us out of prison into a new freedom.

Forgiveness has two distinct parts to it: it has to be offered, but it also has to be received. We need to explore what both parts mean and how both need practising all through our lives on little issues as well as big ones. Receiving forgiveness, like offering it, is a journey. There are stages which may flow from one to another, come together or overlap, or follow on with a large time interval in between. The stages do not have to be sequential and seldom are, but all stages need to be in place for complete forgiveness to be received, and ultimately reconciliation achieved. There is a danger in describing the stages and reading about them that can make them seem too neat and tidy, as they are far from that in practice. There is an innate messiness in the whole process.

Setting things down sequentially on paper or a screen can be helpful in looking at the ingredients, like those which go into making a cake, but the reality in the kitchen and in our minds is not likely to be so ordered. Some recipes need a precise sequence to be followed for them to work, but the journey of forgiveness can take place in a multitude of ways beginning from a huge variety of places. You and I must make our own journeys beginning from where we are. Your route is particular to you. Your starting point is yours, not mine or someone else's. You will put the ingredients together in your own way and in your own time. What matters most now, this moment, is the direction in which you are heading: that you want to forgive, or at least that you want to want to forgive, and that you are on the journey, on the move. It matters less how far along the journey you have travelled already or how fast you are going. Up to a point, these things will look after themselves, even though our ability as human beings to procrastinate and justify ourselves is endless and we always need to guard against such dangers!

Because forgiveness must be received as well as offered, the process of offering does not of itself mean that the perpetrator of violence is thereby automatically 'forgiven': they have to work at the process of receiving what is offered, which is rightly and necessarily demanding, involving their changing themselves and their outlook. As a result, it may never happen even partially, let alone fully. No one can be made to forgive and no one can be made to receive forgiveness. Not doing so, however, leaves people enslaved.

When Nelson Mandela spoke of the moment of being released from prison after being locked up for 27 years, he said, 'As I walked out the door toward the gate that would lead to my freedom, I knew if I didn't leave my bitterness and hatred behind, I'd still be in prison.' Forgiveness is the word that best describes the process of leaving bitterness and hatred behind. Mandela knew what the PoWs standing before the Vietnam Veterans Memorial knew and countless others have known: the way to be fully out of prison.

In today's world, there seems to be trauma and suffering on every side, not least from civil wars, terrorism, slavery and oppression, but also from more extreme climatic disasters. Civil wars have led to more than 20 million people across four countries facing starvation and famine, with two-thirds of the population of the Yemen not knowing where their next meal would come from.

Then there are the victims of violent and abusive relationships, the broken and damaged, who continue to feel immeasurable suffering. Today there is a greater recognition of the ongoing consequences of trauma as well as a greater encouragement for people to speak about it. This is a huge and very positive advance, as issues are brought more fully into the open to begin to be addressed.

A consequence of this is that many more people are risking speaking about being victims and survivors of abuse than ever before, and finding that they are being heard and believed. This is enabling people, at last, to begin to come to terms with horrors that have haunted them throughout their lives.

Counsellors and those in pastoral relationships with victims of trauma and abuse work with them to assist in the whole process of forgiving, and this may be another reason why now is a good time to look at what it means to start the journey of forgiveness as such a vital part of coming to terms with the past.

What applies to our understanding of forgiveness in the face of extremes of trauma and violence is also true of how forgiveness works with every other level of pain, hurt, damage, anger and guilt. If we do not learn how to forgive others for little acts of wrong, we shall not be able to forgive for bigger acts.

St Francis de Sales used to teach people that they needed to guard against gnats and not just hornets. Some who came to him for advice thought that, while they were quite ready to ward off the threat of much larger and more dangerous hornets, they could ignore the gnats, but St Francis taught them differently. He said that if they did not learn how to be watchful and avoid the little temptations then they would not know how to avoid the bigger ones.

The same truth applies to forgiving. We need to learn to forgive the little acts against us and then we shall be more likely to be able to forgive bigger acts if and when they happen. If we have learnt to develop and practise an attitude and way of forgiveness throughout our lives, then it will stand us in good stead when-ever the need arises in the future, whether it be for smaller or larger issues. This highlights the need for children, especially, to learn such a path as well as the rest of us. Clearly, what we learn, absorb and practise when young stays with us and helps form and shape who we are and who we are becoming. We are all 'work in progress', responding to and maybe learning from what we see and hear and do. If we have learnt and practised the need and way of forgiveness as a child, we are far more likely to put it into use regularly in adulthood.

I recall a mother telling me of one of her attempts to teach her young son to say 'sorry' to his younger brother. 'Oh, Peter,' she said, 'look what you've just done to Tim!' 'So?' he snapped. 'Well,' she said, 'go and say "Sorry" to him.' Peter came back to her fast. 'I was going to,' the young child said, 'but you interrupted me after the first two letters!' Some children are clearly more difficult to teach than others!

While our culture is focusing a great deal now on child abuse and safeguarding issues more generally, including of vulnerable adults, there are other whole swathes of hurt and damage that receive much less attention or acknowledgement but are nonetheless hugely hurtful and harmful. These include bullying, sexual harassment, discrimination, domestic violence, the breakdown of marriage and long-term relationships of all kinds, as well as the ongoing consequences, not least for children and grandchildren, nephews and nieces. All these situations, too, need forgiveness to be both offered and received if relationships are to be healed to any degree, or, if healing is not possible, for those involved at least to move on peacefully. Sometimes those caught up in these damaging experiences know that there are areas which need forgiveness but do not know quite how to explore further that need and, in any case, might not even want to because it all continues to be so deeply upsetting and painful.

Many things can trigger this pain. It might be a word or a comment, or a powerful television or Internet image. These go deep into our imaginations. This is particularly true of those suffering through terrorism. Because of the huge publicity that follows each such attack, there is not only the horror of those most immediately involved, together with their families and friends, but also all those who see or picture accounts of the atrocity and, consequently, find themselves remembering past hurts or trauma done to them or others close to them. For these people, the new atrocity gives further power to the old memory and pain, especially if their experience is still raw because of closeness in time, or because of its similarity in some way or because the earlier hurt has to some degree remained unhealed.

Because we have seen a weakening of the use and familiarity of religious language in more recent years, there is less readiness and ability generally to speak about such issues, which do in part include the realm of forgiveness and its associated vocabulary. The ability to speak may have reduced but the need to do so is no less than it ever was and, instead, may have increased.

This decline of religious language and perspective affects individuals in many other ways too. For example, there is probably less readiness among us to accept some of the responsibility for our wrongdoings, whatever scale they are. There is a tendency for us to justify ourselves in some way or try to explain away what has happened in some other manner, such as laying the responsibility on our genes or our upbringing or putting it on to someone else. This tendency is exacerbated by our prevalent culture of 'blame and shame' and of victimhood.

With media that like to focus on individuals, and social media posts that can go viral in seconds, highlighting a person or situation that was previously unknown, we experience the cult of celebrity in a way not seen by earlier generations. When pictures and comments are circulated so fast, brevity becomes a virtue. In such circumstances, views and expressions are far more likely to be direct and extreme and often stated in a way that polarizes. Nuance and subtlety, niceties and courtesy, have little place in a world which wants instant comment and reaction rather than measured consideration and reflection. Complexity and depth are not the coinage. In the more simplistic extremes, shame and blame are at one end of the spectrum and celebrity at the other. But the positions are not fixed but fluid. There are too many examples of individuals moving dramatically from one end of the scale to the other.

There is sometimes a gratuitous delight when a celebrity or person in public life is accused of a wrongdoing. In an instant, with or without evidence, public opinion is roused, and social media become full of comments and expletives blaming, shaming and condemning. It is hard not to see this in part as a projection of unacknowledged guilt leading to a consequential scapegoating and outpouring of self-righteousness. If we do not acknowledge, at least to ourselves, something of our own failings and weaknesses, and if we do not then also admit to at least some of the responsibility for such thoughts and actions, then, like a swarm of gnats, they pile up until the weight of them loads us down. Once this has happened, like the scales going past their tipping point, the burden may well be thrown somewhere else, away from us and on to another. Perhaps this lies at the root of trolling and other vitriol poured out on social media networks. It also highlights the need for us to live the way of forgiveness in order to be healthy as individuals and as a society.

Forgiveness always has a corporate dimension. Some people think that our relationships are private in every way, but that seems to be based on a view that as human beings we are somehow compartmentalized. In practice, what happens to me in any relationship leaves some kind of mark on who I am, even if the mark is minute. If I show an act of kindness to someone, that makes me more able and likely to do so again, either to that person or someone else: it affects me, who I am, what kind of person I am becoming. Similarly, if I lose my temper or tell a lie or deceive someone, I am more likely to do so again in similar circumstances. Once more, I am very slightly, minutely perhaps, a different person from who I was before I lost my temper, lied or deceived. I have changed, even if it is imperceptible to others.

This means that what happens in any one relationship has consequences that might affect how I behave in other relationships because each one contributes to shaping who I am and who I am becoming. For this reason, the distinction that our politicians and others like to make between public and private life is based on a compartmentalized view of human nature which does not do justice to our integrated and complex reality, nor does it recognize that throughout our lives we are all constantly changing. To put it bluntly, if a person lies to their husband or wife, they are more likely to lie to others. If they cheat on a friend, they are more likely to deceive others. If they fiddle tax returns or misuse their expense account, they are less likely to notice or care for the poor and needy.

There is a corporate and social dimension to all relationships and networks. Every action has unforeseen as well as unrecognized consequences. Most of these will be miniscule, some more significant, a few even life-changing. The miniscule ones will eventually mount up and have an accumulative effect. You can see from the way the trees grow on the sea cliffs which way the wind has been blowing them over the years.

For this reason, if as individuals we can learn, especially as children, more about the journey of forgiveness and put it into practice in our situations, then there will be a consequence for others as well as ourselves because we shall become changed people, which in turn will change our relationships to others. If enough people were to do this, then we should see a change in society itself so that our culture became more forgiving. Correspondingly, if we continue to be less familiar with the language and practice of forgiveness and forgiving, and less willing or able to accept responsibility for and acknowledge our faults and failings, then that too will change how our society evolves.

There are social dimensions to forgiveness in other ways as well. If an organization or group or even nation took action that it subsequently viewed as being wrong, could it, or should it, apologize and ask for forgiveness? Or if it was wronged by another corporate group, could it, or should it offer forgiveness? If so, how and by whom should it be expressed? Such questions are raised by issues such as slavery and the wealth that accrued from it, by war and empire, by boundary exclusions and the forming of national borders, and a whole host of other issues from our past. These are questions to be explored more fully later, but to raise them here makes the point that forgiveness matters at every level of society, for individuals, of course, but also for groups, organizations, institutions and the nation itself.

It is also vital to acknowledge the possible or likely consequences of not forgiving. We have recognized already the tragic number of civil wars and other conflicts within the world. So often the seeds of these are laid years, if not centuries, earlier by remembered, half-remembered or even wrongly inculcated injustices and unresolved conflicts, with memories passed down within families and communities, or within tribes and nations. One injustice, real or imagined, can lead so easily to another. One unforgiven and unresolved act can lead to revenge, which in its turn leads to more revenge. The spiral of conflict is all too familiar and real. The opportunity and capacity to blame, to stoke and harbour bitterness, seems immeasurable. Small wonder when this dynamic is at work so forcefully that violence flares and more horrors are committed. The tentacles spread across time as well as communities.

The spiral and cycle of conflict need breaking otherwise, like fire, they become all-consuming. International courts and justice play their part but can be regarded as the preserve of the victors who write the history and make the rules. While that might be held by impartial witnesses and bodies to be wholly untrue in a particular situation, it is nevertheless an extremely difficult perception to dislodge once it has gained traction. Perceptions matter. Fake news has an influence.

The only sure route out of the spiral of escalating violence and revenge is to choose to relinquish the desire for revenge and seek the way of forgiveness and being forgiven.

Before going further, it might be apposite to ask whether forgiveness itself is the right word to be using at all for individuals or society. One person expressed to me the view that the word 'forgiveness' is too heavy and serious. But is that because those who hold that view are reluctant to face up to the weight and seriousness of what we as human beings can do, or is it because there are ways other than forgiveness that will deliver us out of prison? Is acceptance, for example, up to the job? Perhaps, when we come to look at the nature of forgiveness, it will become clearer whether there are other routes, other ways and journeys that can be made as successfully. Suffice it to say here that acceptance can take us on a very important part of the journey, but still only a part. It focuses on how we live with our own history and past and our memory of it, but says nothing about how, in the light of that, we relate to the others who have been involved with us, particularly those who have been the cause, in some degree, of the hurt and harm that has come to us. Forgiveness, on the other hand, not only allows us to accept our past but to move on positively from it. It addresses how we relate to, and engage now and in the future with, those from our past who have done us wrong.

When we consider the part that forgiveness plays in the way of reconciliation, or at least the possibility of establishing some kind of peace or Shalom, then it is evident that there needs to be something positive passing from one to another, not just the neutrality of 'acceptance'. After all, it is possible to accept grudgingly or indifferently as well as positively, and it might say little or nothing about how we then relate to the one who has offended us.

Not forgiving leaves us ultimately imprisoned. It also causes harm and pain along the way. Think, for example, of any close relationship. Being the people we are with our own wishes, ideas and personalities, there is likely to come a time when something that another person says or does is contrary to what we want. In some relationships and with some personalities this will be a frequent occurrence; in others rarer, but it will still happen. When it does happen, at the very least we may feel some irritation or annoyance. Some counsellors will speak about 'pinch points'.[3] If these are ignored or buried, they will build up like drops of water, eventually filling and overflowing the bucket. They won't go away on their own. Acknowledging the pinching, apologizing, talking about it and being open with the other, gives the possibility of finding a way forward to resolve the issue whether small or large. Not doing so will store up trouble for the future so that one pinch point adds to another until a 'crunch' is reached and the relationship is threatened with breakage. Healing and forgiveness can still take place, but they will be more difficult to achieve because the harm done has been greater. Like everything else in our relationships, something caught and addressed at an early stage is easier to put right.

Forgiveness is not just for the bigger issues in our lives but for all the smaller ones too. It may happen with very little needing to be said or done, providing that all of those involved acknowledge at some level what is taking place and do not just skate over or ignore the issue, pretending that apology and forgiveness have happened when they haven't.

It is quite possible for a relationship to function for some long time, perhaps years, without any proper apologies or forgiveness but, in those circumstances, it is likely that the relationship eventually will become more and more limited, perhaps superficial or even dysfunctional, like being out on a war-torn hillside where there are unexploded mines. If there is a proliferation in the number of mines, eventually any safe space will become more and more limited. In terms of relationships, the consequences of not dealing with the potentially explosive issues, and defusing them through forgiveness, is either to accept implicitly that there are increasingly restricted spheres of the relationship with large 'no-go areas' or else risk over-stepping a line, going into unsafe territory and prompting an explosive reaction which may cause serious and irreparable damage. Some relationships and personalities can live with a cycle of small explosions and rows, but for others this would be simply anathema, a series of little deaths. Those relationships which seem to cope with rows may suffer more damage long term than they realize.

Damaged relationships not only affect individuals but also groups within society. If there has been a racial attack, for example, with no adequate response from civic or national leaders, then the racial group that has suffered will feel aggrieved, and doubly hurt, once by the attack and then by the lack of proper condemnation of the attack or support for those hurt. Other vulnerable minority groups are also likely to identify with the suffering of the racial group attacked, as well as those in society who want to stand up against such atrocities wherever and whenever they occur, irrespective of who is responsible for them. A total or partial lack of naming the outrage for what it is, and seeking justice for those harmed, will damage society and threaten to fragment it in a way that is akin to the damage inflicted on any relationship by a lack of forgiveness. So long as the racial attack goes uncondemned, and the minority concerned is not given justice, then all future attacks will make the hurts from the first attack resurface, with the consequent angers fuelling among some the desire for revenge. Past hurts, unresolved injustices and failure to walk the journey of forgiveness will add to the minefield and risk future explosions. This can continue from one generation to another. Society, like individual relationships and those in families, needs forgiveness. However, it also needs to be recognized that both individuals and groups can be hurt and damaged by a genuine accident or even innocent action, yet perceive, wrongly, that their hurt was caused by negligence or worse. In such circumstances, they may want or demand an apology which in fact is not appropriate or possible. There then has to be some attempt to enable the individual or group to see that, while they have been hurt, they have not been wronged in the way they imagine. Similarly, a person may feel hurt because they have misunderstood both what is happening and the motives of others, rather than being actually slighted or wronged.

There are two groups institutionally that may well seek to discourage people from making an apology or asking for forgiveness. In both cases they do so because of how they think it might be interpreted subsequently in a court of law. It used to be common practice for insurance companies and lawyers to instruct their clients not to admit responsibility, for example if they were involved in a car accident, and so not even to apologize in case the apology was taken as an admission of liability. As we know, saying 'sorry' can in fact mean a good many different things. It might mean, 'It was totally my fault and I am very sorry for having driven so badly and damaged your car', or it might mean, 'I am so sorry that you are hurt but it was entirely your fault.' Consequently, a website currently advises:

> In the wake of a car accident, the word 'sorry' should not be part of your vocabulary ... Saying sorry immediately after the accident can complicate the investigation that follows ... For a lot of us, it's hard not to say sorry when we're inconveniencing another person. Realistically, saying sorry doesn't accomplish anything.

This shows an interesting use of the word 'realistically', to say nothing of the view that saying sorry doesn't accomplish anything!

In very different circumstances, such as when someone in an organization is accused of abuse or sexual harassment or negligence, the legal advice can be similar because, in the lawyers' view, apologizing might be seen as admitting liability and so increase the likelihood of the company or organization being found guilty of the offence and liable for damages.

In some situations, of course, it can be that receiving an apology is what the complainant primarily wants rather than financial compensation. In such circumstances, heeding the insurers' or lawyers' advice might be more likely to bring about exactly the situation that they are keen to avoid, namely a claim against them. This is not to be seen, though, as a matter of encouraging an apology as a means of avoiding a financial settlement but rather because apologizing and asking to be forgiven are right in themselves.

A mediator described meeting a woman who was planning to go back to court for a seventh time with her former husband over the issues surrounding their divorce settlement. He asked her why she was going and what she wanted. She replied simply, 'More money'. He expressed surprise at this, saying that in his experience so many court appearances ate money rather than produced it for either party and that maybe there was something else at stake at a deeper and more personal level. When the woman challenged him as to what he thought this might be, he said that perhaps what she really wanted was to hear her former husband say that for the most part she had been a good wife, that they had had a good marriage for many years and that he was genuinely sorry that it had ended badly. The woman started crying and said that if she heard those words from him she would never go to court or bother him again.

Perhaps the advice of some lawyers not to apologize is itself born out of our Western adversarial legal system, which is rather different from some other parts of the world, such as Japan where apologizing is expected promptly as part of social relations and behaviour. Apologizing helps restore social harmony.

Groups such as insurers and lawyers who are known or thought to discourage people from apologizing contribute to the overall attitude of society. It makes saying sorry and seeking forgiveness less likely in some situations. It also gives those who are already wary of apologizing a further reason or excuse not to do so. Furthermore, if a culture becomes more litigious, then it is likely to be one that finds apologizing even harder as people become more conscious of the perceived risk of an apology opening the way to a claim for compensation.

Any increased tendency or reason not to forgive would have far-reaching consequences and cause enormous damage at every level of society. It is hard enough for most of us to apologize and forgive without any additional leverage or reason not to do so.

There was an extraordinary story that came out of the Rwandan genocide of the 1990s. Among the hundreds of thousands of victims and subsequent refugees was a Tutsi woman whose children had been massacred in front of her, along with others from her village, and she had been powerless to stop the atrocity. Now she was in a refugee camp and unable to speak, despite the safety, food and shelter that the camp provided. Eventually, after weeks of living with her nightmares, she was able to stammer out to one of the aid workers, 'There is no forgiveness for my unforgivingness.' Surely, she is right about the seriousness of not forgiving but wrong, we hope, that it cannot be forgiven.

Forgiveness matters to each of us as individuals in every relationship as well as corporately in our different groups, organizations, networks and society as a whole. Not only do we all mess up to some degree or other, but those we know and with whom we are involved do it to us at times. In addition, there are the more extreme experiences and horrors from which people can suffer. So, we need a route out of the consequences of our actions, as well as a way out for those damaged by the actions of others, be they slight or great.

But what is this route? What is forgiveness?

2

What is forgiveness?

If someone wrongs us in some way, we might feel offended, resentful or even vengeful. The scale of the wrong can, of course, vary enormously from the trivial to something major. The response from us can vary enormously, too. If a stranger pushes in front of you in a queue or makes a derogatory comment about your dress or your hair, then you may be irritated or annoyed but are unlikely to pursue the matter or lose too much sleep over it. If, however, the same comment about your appearance is made by your spouse or best friend, or repeated daily, then it takes on a very different significance and is likely to evoke a very different response. The words themselves, therefore, are not the only issue: who says them and in what way or context and with what frequency also matter. A person may react slightly when someone pushes in at a checkout but feel road rage if it is a car at traffic lights.

If the wrong done to you is far greater, such as someone striking you or breaking into your home and stealing from you, then your natural response of anger, outrage, resentment or retaliation may well come to the fore, whether the offence was committed by someone you knew or not. If the affront was from someone you knew, the hurt would be greater and the response even more marked. The Psalmist understood this all too well:

> It is not enemies who taunt me –
>   I could bear that;
> it is not adversaries who deal insolently with me –
>   I could hide from them.
> But it is you, my equal,
>   my companion, my familiar friend,
> with whom I kept pleasant company.[1]

In addition to the scale and nature of the injury, a response will also be dependent upon other very different factors, such as the character, history, experience, temperament, outlook, values and state of the person who has been the victim.

In the face of such complexity, what part can and does forgiveness play and how does it relate to this vast range of other responses? What does forgiveness mean?

Forgiveness is a familiar enough word to most people, and yet it is far from straightforward to define. Indeed, there are those who think that it is better not to try because it means so many different things to different people, and even different things to the same person at different times, depending upon the circumstances.

In her essay, 'As Mysterious as Love', at the start of *The Forgiveness Project*, Marina Cantacuzino explains why she has chosen not to define forgiveness:

> The only thing I know for sure is that the act of forgiving is fluid and active and can change from day to day, hour to hour, depending on how you feel when you wake in the morning or what triggers you encounter during the day.

As Marina Cantacuzino says, the process of forgiving itself can change from day to day, so trying to define the word forgiveness may not be very helpful to some, especially to those most deeply in the throes of struggling to forgive. Also, a genuine act of forgiveness, done in good faith, may be overtaken or reversed because the feelings of the person forgiving have changed. In the face of such fluidity, a definition can seem far too static, cold, analytical and even prescriptive. At other times, being able to say what forgiveness can be provides something of a goal and target to work towards. Also, it can be of assistance to those supporting or working with others who are struggling to forgive. On a journey, it is helpful to have some picture of the hoped-for destination, and a clue as to the route.

Dictionaries are likely to tell us that forgiveness means 'to pardon' or 'to remit'. Fuller definitions take us further, such as 'no longer feel angry about or wish to punish', and this is certainly a key part of what the word means at its best and fullest.

The responses to wrongs done to us, while fully understandable, are likely to be negative: at the weaker end, irritation or annoyance; at the stronger end, anger, resentment, vengefulness or retaliation. Forgiveness, in part, addresses these negative responses by seeking to set them aside, to overcome them, or at least not be controlled by them. Deborah van Deusen Hunsinger in *Forgiveness and Truth* captures this dimension with her definition: 'Forgiveness means relinquishing all retributive emotions and all desires to retaliate.'[2] This is a much more expressive statement of overcoming the negative dimension than the straightforward dictionary definitions. Another expression of trying to end the negative aspects of forgiveness is quoted by the American actress Lily Tomlin, though it is unclear quite where the words originated: 'Forgiveness means giving up all hope for a better past.' John Monbourquette, in his book *How to Forgive*, writes that 'The first step on the long road to forgiveness is the decision to not seek revenge'.[3]

If it is possible to overcome to some degree or even fully our initial negative response to an offence, then what replaces that first response? It is at this point that most of the definitions of forgiveness seem limited or silent. The absence of negative emotions, feelings or thoughts do not just leave a vacuum. They will be replaced either with something essentially neutral, such as indifference, or else by something more positive. The possibilities are enormous, just as for the possible range of initial negative responses. Forgiveness needs to say something about these possibilities that follow on from seeking to set aside the negative. Vacuums are not natural. Something fills them. The question is 'What?' Forgiveness needs to direct us towards what *replaces* the negative. In other words, any complete definition and understanding of forgiveness must include both a negative and a positive part. At its best, *forgiveness is not only giving up our desire for revenge but also, ultimately, wanting the other's good rather than their harm.*

If this seems too much to ask of those who have been horrendously hurt, it is important to recognize that the statement is a goal for the journey. Wanting the other's good may never completely come about, but is set over against wanting the other's harm or desiring to get even with them. There is a whole spectrum of possibilities of wanting the other's good, with many possible developments along the journey. It does not commit a person to actively seek that good, though that always remains an option and even an ideal. Furthermore, as will become more apparent, it is aspirational – a work in progress – especially when trauma has been suffered. No one expects a positive response initially, indeed quite the contrary. We are all likely to have our initial response to wrongs done to us somewhere in the range of the negative reactions already considered. Forgiveness comes later, if at all, and only by being worked at can it be achieved. But the aspiration for something positive to take over from the negative is an important goal. Neutrality is not enough, because indifference to other people will always seem cold and negative.

Acceptance tends to be warmer and more positive than indifference but can still be relatively neutral. While there can be a wholehearted acceptance, there can also be a grudging acceptance. Acceptance speaks more of finding a way to live with what has happened than it does about addressing any underlying issues.

Our word *forgive* comes from the Old English *forgiefan*, which in its turn looks back to the Latin *perdonare*. While our word *pardon* clearly has the same root as the Latin, 'pardon' and 'forgive' have diverged in their contemporary meanings, though both keep the sense of something being *given*, which is inherently positive. Because pardon has both the legal dimension of remission of a punishment for a crime and the slighter usage in common speech of 'begging someone's pardon', it is no longer synonymous with forgiveness.

The aspect of gift is clearly present in the meaning of forgiving a debt and in that sense waiving it. The word was used extensively in this way at the beginning of the new millennium, with all the discussion about forgiving the national debts of the world's most highly indebted nations as part of the Jubilee. This use of language remains highly pertinent, not only in terms of the continuing need to help the poorest of the world, but also because it invites us to look at offences done to us as debts that need forgiving. We shall explore this dimension more later on, but to see offences as stealing something from us, and thereby creating a debt that needs repaying, can be a helpful way to understand something of what has happened when we have been badly wronged and damaged. There is so much that can be stolen beyond material things, perhaps especially our self-esteem and confidence, our ability to trust others and forge deep or lasting relationships, joy and happiness, carefree giving, spontaneity. It also needs recognizing, however, that someone may end up in actual financial debt, not because of their own wrong but through theft or extortionate interest rates, for example. The same is true for nations.

A young man called Darren tells of his being sexually abused by a teacher whom he trusted. Indeed, the man had been 'grooming' him and asked him and some other boys to stay on after school to help with a project. Although Darren says that the abuse was not extreme and was restricted to one evening, the consequences and damage stayed with him for years after. He felt great shame, blamed himself and would not tell anyone about it, least of all his parents. He found that he no longer trusted any adults, especially the other teachers, and this affected everything in his schooling as well as other relationships. Trust had been stolen from him. Although it was to return when he later learnt to forgive, the years could not be rolled back and the lost educational opportunities could not be replaced.

Offending and damaging another person will always contain the dimension of theft, of taking away something that can never completely be returned. Forgiveness works to overcome some of these consequences. It is about giving rather than stealing, healing rather than damaging, restoring rather than destroying.

The root association of forgiveness with giving highlights the need for the positive dimension of any definition of forgiveness. It also encourages the sense of generosity that will always be in forgiveness. The person offering forgiveness does not have to do so. Forgiveness can never be a right or requirement. It is always something offered, given freely, chosen, which is also why in the Christian tradition it is associated with *grace*. One of the words used in the Greek of the New Testament for forgive is *charizomai*, which, in addition to the sense of forgiving freely, carries the meaning of giving or granting. Its root comes from the word *charis*, which can be translated as grace as well as a kindness, benefit, free gift, thankfulness even. No wonder that forgiveness needs a positive dimension in its definition!

The principal word for forgiveness in the Greek of the New Testament in the Gospels is *aphiēmi*, with its sense of *letting go* or *sending from*. This is a different emphasis both from the generous, gracious giving of *charizomai*, and also the core root Latin of *donare*, *giving*, which is present in the definition of forgiveness in most of the European languages of today. *Aphiēmi* clearly reflects the same essential truth of how to move on from negative responses to something more positive, and is expressed in Deborah van Deusen Hunsinger's word *relinquishing*. It speaks of *separation*, *detachment*, putting something away and sending it out of reach.

Both the giving of *charizomai* and the letting go of *aphiēmi* need to be conscious choices in the one who is forgiving. They are not arrived at by accident nor are they simply a feeling inside us, though it may well be a response to extremely strong feelings and emotions that is the spur. Forgiveness itself always needs to be a choice or decision, though just as forgiveness is a journey, so too is the choice or decision to forgive. It is not all or nothing. It is probably not arrived at instantly but is a gradual and uneven journey. That is not to imply that a person deliberately chooses to 'half forgive' but rather that wanting to forgive, or at least wanting to want to forgive, takes time because their pain and other reactions within them continue to hold them back. However, emotions or feelings are not enough: there always needs to be this dimension of the will.

We have seen a huge shift in emphasis culturally from the mind to the heart, from thoughts to feelings, in how we make decisions, relate to one another, speak of ourselves. Many who might in the past have begun expressing a view or opinion with the words, 'I think …' are now more likely to say, 'I feel …'. What follows may be no different, whatever the introductory words, but the appeal is now to our feelings rather than our rational thought. Feelings seem more acceptable within our post-Enlightenment culture, less easily challenged, less open to being questioned or scrutinized, more empathetic, more personal. By contrast, thoughts can seem colder and distant, impersonal and directive, but also more open to scrutiny, challenge and debate.

As a result, we are more likely to see decisions as being made because of our feelings rather than our thoughts, and risk confusing the two. The truth so often is that both are rightly involved, even if the relationship or balance between them is not always very clear. When two people are married, for example, the minister says to each in turn, 'Will you take N to be your wife/husband?' and each answers, 'I will.' The question is not, 'Do you feel like taking N to be your wife/husband?' with a corresponding answer, 'I feel like it.' This is not to say that the feelings are not deeply involved in the decision to be married, but it is to say that there must also be deliberate choice, an exercising of the will and not just the feelings. What is true of love in marriage is true of the choice to forgive. Love is not *just* a feeling any more than forgiveness is, though it would hardly be love or forgiveness if it involved no feeling.

If the decision to forgive involves us consciously and deliberately not only giving up our desire for revenge but also, ultimately, wanting the other's good, then how does that relate to our feelings as well as our thoughts? It clearly needs to engage both. How it does so will vary enormously from person to person, issue to issue, stage to stage, day to day. As Marina Cantacuzino put it, it is likely to be *fluid*. Sometimes it will be the feelings that lead the thought and sometimes the other way around. In the more extreme cases, when a person finds themselves facing or having faced anger, disgust, revulsion, outrage or shame, the journey to forgive, if it starts at all, is more likely to do so with the will than with the feelings, and then only very tentatively.

In trying to be clearer about what forgiveness itself *is*, looking at what it *is not* can assist the process. It is very definitely not condoning or excusing. The offence is the offence. The offender is the offender. There will be reasons why he or she said or did what they did, even if they themselves do not immediately know them. There may be mitigating issues or circumstances, but that is a world away from condoning or excusing. Only when an offence has been faced up to by the offender, or at least that process has started, can there be the possibility of their realizing its inevitable complexity. Even the slightest offence still needs to be acknowledged by the one who has committed it as an offence that needs forgiving if they are to receive forgiveness. The person offended against may understand more fully and clearly what happened and why, and even seek to reassure the offender that the offence was not totally their fault, but that is not the same as denying that it was an offence or exonerating the person that caused the hurt. Rather, it is likely to be a reaching out to the other to lessen their sense of guilt or shame. Forgiveness is still needed because an offence has taken place.

Just as forgiveness is not condoning or excusing, it is not minimalizing or ignoring. There has always to be a truthful and honest recognition of what has happened. Without that there can be no real progress or development in a relationship. While that may never be sought in cases of horror and trauma, in the majority of occasions when we need to forgive someone it is in the context of some kind of ongoing relationship with them. Bypassing and ignoring uncomfortable experiences is like leaving the landmines unexploded and skirting round them as best we can in a reduced area of relationship. Landmines need to be identified, uncovered, defused and removed. Only then can a relationship grow once more and fulfil its potential.

It is not just related but different words that can distort our understanding of forgiveness: wrong or misleading definitions can do so as well. One definition claims that forgiveness involves a restoration of trust. While that is true up to a point for reconciliation, it is not true of forgiveness. Because of the distinction between forgiveness being offered and forgiveness being received, it is entirely possible for forgiveness to be offered with no acceptance of it at all by the one to whom it is offered and no restoration of relationship whatsoever. Also, it is entirely possible for someone to offer forgiveness but have no wish to see a relationship restored, even if it had been a close one prior to the offence.

Forgiveness does not turn the clock back. It does not mean that everything is back as it was, as though nothing had happened. Forgiveness does make a future possible and can open the door to healing and reconciliation where those are sought mutually. Even then, trust may never be fully restored. In some cases, perhaps trust should not be fully restored, because underlying and unresolved, maybe unresolvable, issues or personality traits, previously unknown or hidden, have come to light.

It takes very many years for a tree to grow and mature though it can be cut down with a chain saw in a matter of minutes.

Similarly, with trust. Once cut it may grow again, slowly, but never as strongly and probably with far smaller, weaker shoots.

Trust cut down by a betrayal of some kind is never likely to grow as strong again. What is more, the behaviour that has led to the betrayal may well have revealed a flaw in the character of the betrayer that is not likely to change soon, if ever. In such circumstances, even if a relationship is in part recoverable, it may well need both parties to help guard against that trait, weakness or flaw. To pretend that it is not there, to fail to face reality, is likely to make the situation worse. In such circumstances, premature trust makes future damage more likely. Premature trust can be misplaced, dangerous and harmful. The restoration of trust at the wrong time in the wrong way is very definitely not a requirement of forgiveness and should be avoided.

The phrase 'forgive and forget' has done a great deal to make forgiving harder for many people. Too often it trips off people's tongues as advice at a time when even beginning the journey of forgiveness is a huge struggle, and forgetting is the last thing a person wants or thinks possible, let alone likely. Some will counter the phrase by saying, 'I may be able to come to forgive but I shall never forget.' In the case of extreme horrors, how can one forget? An experience of evil or trauma is likely to be so strongly and deeply imprinted on a person's memory that they are scarred with it for life, unable to forget even if they wish to do so.

In such circumstances, being told to forgive and forget can make a person think that the two must go together and, since they know that they will never be able to forget, they may assume, wrongly, that they will never be able to forgive either, which can initiate or compound guilt.

As a result, it is crucially important to uncouple the words *forgive* and *forget*. Forgiving can indeed make forgetting more likely or possible, but forgetting can never be made a requirement or expectation. If forgetting happens because you have offered forgiveness, it can be a blessing received but not a requirement. In situations where forgiveness can begin and develop, it is more likely that the hurt and pain associated with the issue lessen, so that it is recalled less frequently. As long as hurts trouble us deeply, they are constantly at the forefront of our minds and can in no way be forgotten. If the matter recedes from our immediate consciousness, then the beginning of forgetting can take place. The more deeply a matter has been imprinted on our memory, which may well be a measure of the scale of its horror, then the less likely it is ever to be forgotten fully. Forgetting, like forgiving itself, is a journey.

As the journey of forgiveness develops, so the journey of forgetting is likely to as well. Furthermore, when the event or events that are being forgiven are still being recalled, they may well be remembered with less associated sense of anguish or need for revenge. Ultimately, it is possible for a person fully to forgive another while still remembering what has happened, but no longer with animosity and with a greatly reduced sense of pain and hurt.

In some cases, even where forgiveness or partial forgiveness has been possible, it is very important that a person does not forget or try to forget. Given the readiness of people to say 'forgive and forget', that may seem a strange statement, but it can be vital for a victim's own protection in the future that they continue to remember, just as it can be vitally important that they do not rush to trust.

Take for example an occasion of domestic violence that was triggered by a combination of events: a husband who had been watching pornographic films in the company of others, all under the influence of drink and drugs, returned home and beat his wife. If she was able subsequently to forgive him, it would be crucially important that neither she nor he forgot what had happened. Both of them, in their different ways, would need to try to ensure that the toxic combination of drink, porn, wrong company and drugs was not allowed to happen again. The husband would need to agree to his wife helping him in this. Both would need to remain vigilant, remembering the past if they were to try to prevent violence in the future. Clearly, it would also be most important for the husband especially to seek counselling and assistance from others, and his wife too, so that they could look and work at underlying issues that caused his violence. This would very definitely need to be a case of forgive and remember, not forgive and forget.

There are a huge number of situations where an offence has been committed because of a particular trigger or combination of triggers, such as alcohol or drugs, a gang or group of friends present, a video or words of a song, online messaging, or an event of some kind. The range is limitless. If a person has been damaged but able to begin the forgiving process, then they may well need to remember in order to avoid the risk of any repeat of what happened previously.

In those circumstances, it is also important that the deliberate recalling of an event for the sake of future protection is not associated with the recall also of bitterness or revenge. That uncoupling is part of what the forgiveness eventually makes possible, but it needs working on, which is back to the will and not just the feelings. 'Forgive and remember' may be better advice than 'Forgive and forget'.

It is important, however, not to use this as justification for deliberately holding on to a memory for some malicious reason. Memories can be used as weapons to throw back at the offender in order to wound and add to their sense of guilt or shame. Memories of deep pain and hurt can also be used intentionally to keep alive hate or revenge that otherwise might lessen. Some people keep mental lists of the faults of others, ready to lob them into a conversation with the aim of exercising some control or power over the other person, or else to justify their own unkind-nesses, at least in their own eyes. We are capable of twisting most things to our own ends if we have a desire to do so.

There is another dimension to the need not to forget. As part of its protection, the mind may temporarily seek to bury or blot out of the memory events that are too painful or with which it is too difficult for it to cope. This can last a short or long time and be associated with a range of conditions, including dissociative amnesia. So long as the not remembering persists, then coming to terms with the event that has triggered it and is now forgotten will not be possible. Forgetting in these circumstances makes forgiving impossible because the person does not know what or who it is that needs forgiving. Anyone suffering from this kind of amnesia is likely to need professional assistance to overcome it.

A complete memory block can also be the result of a victim's denial of what has occurred. This may well be occasioned by the severity of the pain or degradation inflicted on them, com-pounded by the nightmares of questioning self-worth, value and esteem.

Christine was bathing her daughter one evening when she found herself suddenly and unexpectedly crying. She was a happily married mother of three sons as well as her daughter, and had no obvious reason to be sad except that, years earlier, she had been abused. Now she found herself seeing her daughter in all her innocence, vulnerability and happiness. She remembered those qualities in her own childhood and how they had been shattered. Her tears were of the pain of what had been lost, but were also prompted by the wish that her little girl be protected from all that was evil, as she herself had not been. The memory that had been locked away and buried was triggered and released through the love she had for her own daughter.

Extreme trauma and horror can remain buried for many years but resurface totally unexpectedly, perhaps with a combination of a trigger that links to the person's own past and a happier, more secure and settled stage in their life that makes the facing of the horror more possible.

If the deep burying and memory block are for the extremes, in a similar but less total way it is not uncommon for people to experience an initial numbness or freezing of their feelings in the face of the shock of something profoundly upsetting, like hearing very bad news or discovering that their house has been ransacked. This numbness generally wears off naturally with time so that what has occurred can be remembered and reflected upon as the person then chooses.

Sometimes the choice is to leave the most painful memories buried and not to acknowledge or examine them because the recall is too painful and confusing. After the horror of war, for example, combatants and civilian casualties may well not talk at all for many years, if ever, about what has happened to them. In these cases, people are not forgetting because they have forgiven but because they do not know how else to cope. Forgetting is then a protection that becomes a habit, a way of distancing themselves and retreating from the hurt and pain, leaving it undisturbed and seeking to reduce its power to disturb and hurt again.

The fiftieth anniversary of the end of the Second World War acted as a trigger for many who had been involved in the fighting to speak about it, often for the first time. This was partly because of the media coverage, partly the result of hearing others speak or in response to the questions of family or friends, but also because it *was* 50 years and the horrors and memories were accordingly less intense.

Because memory plays a key role in helping to protect victims from repeat situations, or comparable ones, I was surprised to discover that *The Anchor Yale Bible Dictionary* gives as a definition of forgiveness, 'the wiping out of an offense from memory'.[4] While that can sometimes happen as a result of forgiveness, it is certainly not always a consequence and sometimes deliberately should not be allowed to be, as we have been exploring.

While looking at what forgiveness is not can help clarify what it is, so also looking at responses not so different from forgiveness itself can aid our understanding. We have referred already to the fact that pardon has the same root in Latin as the word forgive but has diverged nevertheless in its meaning. In a similar way, the word 'amnesty' links in meaning with 'forgetting', yet has diverged from it and come closer to pardoning. It is likely to apply especially in political situations where wrongs have been recognized, culpability apportioned and sentences passed down by the courts. It can also apply to police or other authorities giving notice that, for a fixed period of time, they will not take action against a specific offence, such as possessing a weapon, in order to encourage people to hand in their weapons for the benefit of themselves and the whole community.

Another word akin to forgiveness is 'remission', which, from its Latin root, is literally a sending back or restoring. Like forgiveness, it is associated with debt relief but also the remission of time spent in prison because of good behaviour.

Perhaps a word and idea closer to the meaning of forgiveness is that of showing mercy. It carries with it something of the positive element of forgiveness as well as the removal of the negative. At one level, it is about showing leniency, clemency and compassion, but we also use the word as in the phrase 'being thankful for small mercies'. The dimension that links it with gratitude is also there in the French word for thank you.

Mercy is a quality that can be shown by a person or body such as a court. Although mercy is concerned with punishment, like forgiveness it is a gift. Shakespeare has Portia famously speak of this in *The Merchant of Venice*: 'The quality of mercy is not strained. It droppeth as the gentle rain from heaven upon the place beneath.' No forcing. No requiring. Gift. Grace. Mercy is seen as a heavenly and royal quality, something to which to aspire, 'an attribute to God himself'.

The appeal for mercy and pardon is an appeal to overrule what has been handed down from a court. Whether the court's judgement was just or not might be a moot point, but if a pardon is given then the sentence is set aside. Even in these circumstances it begs the question about the relationship of a pardon to justice, and, more widely, the relationship of forgiveness to justice.

There are those who will not forgive because, they say, forgiving would mean that the person who has offended me would 'get off scot-free'. Once again, this is based on a misunderstanding of the nature of forgiveness. Offering forgiveness does not mean that a person is forgiven until they are able to receive it. As we shall see later, that requires their trying to restore at least some of what has been damaged or taken, as well as ensuring that justice has been done where the offence concerned involved a criminal act. The offer of forgiveness may be total and free, yet full acceptance by the offender will require their repentance and restitution. The offer of forgiveness may not be conditional but the full receiving will be. There are always questions about the nature of justice itself, not least, 'Whose justice?' However, the attempt to ensure that justice is done, and has been done, belongs with the due process of receiving forgiveness and is in no way jeopardized by the offering of forgiveness.

Throughout this consideration of the meaning of forgiveness as giving up our desire for revenge and ultimately coming to a point of wanting the other's good, we have seen that forgiveness is relational and focused on the person who has offended, not the offence that they have committed. It is people who need forgiving, not events.

Some*thing* that has happened to us can be completely wrong and evil, something that should never have taken place. It can have caused huge harm and still be doing so. We can regret it totally and profoundly and certainly wish with all our being that it had never occurred. We can hate it as an event and feel nothing but repugnance at the recollection of it. Nevertheless, it remains an event, caused by a human being or beings, at least in part. The event is something that eventually we have to come to terms with as part of our own history, as fact. It itself cannot be forgiven, since forgiveness is directed at a person not a thing. It remains and will for ever remain wrong, harmful, evil perhaps. We cannot 'give up our desire for revenge' on something inanimate, nor 'want their good rather than harm'. The person or people associated with what has happened, and to some degree responsible for it, are a very different matter. We may wish with all our heart that we had never had any dealings with them, or they with us, but tragically we have. In that sense, at least, they relate to us and now need our forgiveness.

If there is a knife stabbing in the street, it is not the action of the knife wounding someone that needs the forgiving but the hand of the person holding it: they are responsible. If a car veers off its carriageway and smashes into an oncoming vehicle, it is not the car that needs forgiving but the driver who was distracted by sending a text message: it is he or she who is responsible.

It is always we *people* who carry responsibility. It is we who need forgiving.

To risk forgiving and reach out in some degree, however small, towards another person who has wronged us in some way is to work towards the restoration of relationship. If our offer is received, even welcomed, then something has changed between us.

Forgiveness is always relational. Our offering forgiveness frees us from the imprisonment of bitterness and revenge. Our receiving forgiveness has the power to renew and release us.

Most of the hurts and harms done to us are by people who we know, probably friends or family since they are closest to us and are able, consequently, to hurt us most easily and we them. Because we care more, we are more open. Because we are more open, we are more vulnerable. Because we are more vulnerable, we are more easily taken advantage of and hurt.

When these close relationships become estranged or damaged, if we offer forgiveness and it is received, then a new level of relating can begin. It may be very weak, wary and initially hesitant, or it may be a much quicker and stronger restoration. However it is, it will be about two people who were distant having the potential to grow close again, maybe even to flourish, sometimes to become stronger in their relationship than they were before, reaching a new level of honesty and understanding both with one another and with themselves, experiencing more deeply than ever the care, acceptance and love one for another. In these cases, the gifts of offering and receiving forgiveness are a delight, grace, the means to a deeper, more meaningful and joyful quality of life.

3

Who can forgive?

The short answer to the question, 'Who can forgive?' is, of course, everyone. We can all offer and receive forgiveness. We all *need* to offer and receive forgiveness. But who can we forgive, and who can we not forgive?

The dozen or so members of a church house group that met weekly for a year or more knew one another very well. One Sunday, Peter came to the church for the first time. Some of the house group members were talking to him after the service and invited him to join them that week for their meeting, which he duly did. He started to attend regularly. After he had been going for three months or so and felt himself accepted by others, he told them at the end of one of their meetings that there was something he would like them to know about himself. He began to tell them how he had been in prison until recently, having been convicted of child abuse. He said how much he regretted everything that he had done, that he had paid the price and moved on. It would never happen again. He had changed, and he wanted the other members of the group to know, so that he could be open and truthful with them. He said how important it was to him that they not only knew what he had done but were able to accept him and let him continue to be part of their group. They were all very silent and shocked as they listened. He had seemed so 'nice and normal'.

When they met the following week, the leader of the group began by telling Peter that all the others had had an extra meeting without him to talk about what he had told them and that they had decided to forgive him. He also said that they would, of course, need to inform the Parish Safeguarding Officer who would then need to meet with Peter to draw up a formal Agreement saying what he would and wouldn't be permitted to do in the church. Peter said how grateful he was for their forgiveness and understanding and how much that helped him. The meeting then continued as usual.

Were the house group members right to forgive Peter? He had not needed to say anything to them but had been open with them voluntarily, truthfully as far as they could tell. He had expressed remorse, served his time in prison and said he had changed. Did they have any right to forgive him? If not, what should they have said or done?

Forgiveness can only be offered by those who have themselves suffered in some way through the actions of the one to be forgiven, when they have something specific to forgive. In Peter's situation, great harm had been done by him, but not directly or even indirectly to the members of the house group. While he had committed serious offences, they were not the ones offended against, other than as fellow citizens and, in that sense, part of the wider community that is always going to be damaged and weakened by serious wrongdoing and law breaking. As a result, there was nothing expressly for them personally to forgive, though plenty for Peter's victim or victims and their families to forgive if they chose to do so.

The desire of the house group members to welcome Peter and encourage and strengthen the changes that he said had taken place in him was itself good but had led to confusion about the nature of forgiveness. Their response to Peter also failed to understand sufficiently the nature of child abuse and what the Lucy Faithfull Foundation[1] and others working in that field describe as the *distorted thinking* of abusers. It can be dangerous to accept too readily a person's assurance that they have changed, not because of being unduly suspicious but because it is right to be questioning, to be properly and *responsibly suspicious*. The nature of abuse and the characteristic need of the abuser to find others who will help reinforce their distorted thinking is increasingly understood. It must be guarded against, primarily for any victim's or future victim's sake, but also for the abuser's own sake, since without their distorted thinking and self-deception being challenged they remain a danger to others and to themselves.

Over against this, there is the huge need for a circle of support, friendship and reinforcing of right thinking of those who have managed to change or are genuinely seeking to change. Without that circle of support the danger of slipping back into former habits and relationships with other abusers is all the greater. Those who have dealings with sex offenders and abusers need to try to know what their actual state of mind is, not just what they claim it to be. Misplaced trust will do harm. Failure to show trust when it is appropriate will also do harm.

Clearly the house group only had Peter's own word about his changed attitude; they needed far more information and evidence about his situation so that they could be clearer as to how best to respond to what he was saying. They needed to ask his permission to be in touch with others who knew him and could vouch for what he was saying. This is never a comfortable stance for us to take. We may appear to be unduly suspicious rather than properly vigilant, responsibly checking out the facts in a serious situation where the wrong response will do further harm. If Peter had genuinely changed, as he said he had, he would be likely to understand the group's concern and desire for corroboration of his account. Indeed, he will want to help them find it, so that he really could receive their genuine acceptance, encouragement and help. Whatever else they discovered, however, would still not make it right or appropriate for them to express forgiveness; that was not theirs to give.

If Peter had not changed his thinking as much as he was suggesting he had, then hearing words of forgiveness, whether inappropriate or not, would have been likely to make him a greater danger to children and to himself because it would have strengthened his distorted view of the world.

Not only, therefore, was it wrong for the house group members to have expressed forgiveness when they had no right to do so, it was also potentially dangerous.

The attitude of the house group was an example of what the German pastor and theologian Dietrich Bonhoeffer wrote about as 'cheap grace'. In *The Cost of Discipleship*, he said, 'Cheap grace is the preaching of forgiveness without requiring repentance.'[2] A few pages later, and with some irony, he writes, 'Of course you have sinned, but now everything is forgiven, so you can stay as you are and enjoy the consolation of forgiveness.' That is the very particular danger of pronouncing words of forgiveness prematurely and far too easily. Bonhoeffer writes of it as a 'fatal misunderstanding','the bitterest foe of discipleship, which true discipleship must loathe and detest'.[3]

While Bonhoeffer's essay goes on to speak very explicitly about the dangers of cheap grace for Christian disciples (hence the title of his book), the dangers are universal and need to be heeded by all people.

The question of who has the right to forgive another is raised very sharply by the Austrian, Simon Wiesenthal, in his book *The Sunflower*. At the outbreak of the Second World War, Wiesenthal and his wife were living in Lvov. In late 1941, they were moved out of the ghetto where they had been living and sent first to Janowska Concentration Camp and then to other camps. They both survived the war and Wiesenthal devoted much of his life afterwards to tracking down and helping to bring to justice Nazi war criminals.

In *The Sunflower*, Wiesenthal writes of how, when he was in the Lemberg Concentration Camp in 1943, he was summoned to the bedside of a dying Nazi soldier, Karl Seidl. The soldier told him of a crime that he had committed a year earlier, the destruction of a house full of 300 Jews. Before he died, Seidl wanted to be forgiven by a Jew for the crime he had committed. Wiesenthal writes of how he listened to the Nazi soldier and then left his room without saying anything. He then poses the question of whether or not to forgive Seidl. In the original edition of the book, ten different people individually and separately wrote their answers. A further 43 additional answers were included in a later edition. The responses came from a wide range of people, with very different religious and cultural backgrounds, many of whom had themselves suffered. The majority (34) of those who gave a response decided that it was not right to forgive.

It is hard to see how any individual who was not involved with the Jews that Karl Seidl killed could forgive him for their deaths. They might want him to be forgiven, or they might be able to pronounce forgiveness in God's name, but not in their own.

When Emperor Hirohito of Japan died in 1989, attendance at his funeral by world dignitaries was controversial. It was attended by many members of royal families, prime ministers and other dignitaries from around the world. 166 countries were invited to send representatives and all but three did. However, for many of the countries it was no easy decision who should attend in their name. The new American President Bush was there but not the Prime Minister of Australia. Prince Philip went from the UK together with Geoffrey Howe, the Foreign Secretary, but not without criticism from some of the war veterans from the Far East and others. An Anglican bishop was reported to have said that it was 'a gross moral insensitivity' for Prince Philip to attend. At the time, it was also suggested that forgiveness was, or was in danger of being, confused with political expediency.

At issue in part was the role that Emperor Hirohito had played during the Second World War and in the time immediately before it. One view was that the Emperor was a figurehead with little or no control or influence on the political and military leaders and their decision to go to war. The opposing view saw him as having been in a position to influence or even stop the movement towards war and yet failing to do so. With tens of thousands dying in Japanese prisoner of war camps and millions estimated as having been killed in the conflict or dying from disease as a direct result of it, it is small wonder that Emperor Hirohito's death occasioned renewed controversy and tragic memories. It presented governments with difficult decisions as to whom to send to the funeral and how their presence would be interpreted. What message did a government want to convey? How could it do so? How did they balance the competing demands of honouring past memories and upholding economic and diplomatic relations in the present and future? And what about the veterans directly affected by Japanese atrocities, who had already offered forgiveness? How could they be represented or their attitude expressed?

The national debate in Britain made it clear that while many wanted to 'forgive and forget' and 'move on', others did not and thought that we could never forgive since doing so would be a betrayal of those who had died.

Is it ever possible for a nation to forgive another one? If it is, then how is it known when that point is reached? Presumably not everyone has to be in agreement, since that is extremely unlikely ever to happen in our pluralist, international societies. In which case, does it need a majority of a particular size, or is this not about numbers but about an elected government's decision on behalf of its citizens? If so, what would or should form such a decision? Should those who were directly involved, perhaps together with their families, have the determining voice? What if a significant proportion of those families were opposed to forgiveness being expressed but a large majority of other people were in favour? Should there be a right of veto?

If a decision to forgive could ever be reached, then who should express it on behalf of the nation? Should it be our Prime Minister as elected head? Or perhaps the monarch?

If an expression of forgiveness could ever be made and were ever seen to be appropriate, would it relate to whether or not the nation or power being forgiven had expressed any remorse or apology or taken part in reparation of some kind?

In the case of Japan, there have been different levels of apology over the years with the first seemingly having been with China in the 1970s, then the Korean peninsula in the 1980s, although there had been a normalization agreement with the Republic of Korea in 1965, but even as recently as October 2013 the Korean President was still asking for Japan to apologize for its wrongs. However, in August 1995, on the fiftieth anniversary of the end of the Second World War in Asia, the Japanese Cabinet agreed a statement and the Prime Minister stated his 'deep remorse' and 'heartfelt apology' for the 'tremendous damage and suffering caused to the people of many nations'.

If it is highly improbable that any nation could or would reach a point of stating its forgiveness of another nation, there are perhaps a surprising number of bilateral international relations that demonstrate an implicit forgiveness. Singapore and Thailand both had many and extreme reasons to have very strained relationships with Japan, yet both have reached a level of trade and positive international relationship with Japan, which might be regarded as showing an implicit forgiveness. So too the USA now has very positive trade and diplomatic relations, tourism, finance and business links with its former enemy, Japan. It might be pointed out that, long before that, the USA had achieved a 'special relationship' with its former colonial 'enemy', Britain, against which it had waged war, again without any subsequent formal statement of forgiveness or indeed apology in either direction, though that was more than 200 years ago and the wars in question were waged without anything like the level of atrocities seen in the Second World War.

While Japan did make an apology in 1995, which included the USA, along with other nations, there has been no apology for the dropping of a nuclear bomb on Hiroshima or Nagasaki. An argument for those bombs was that, in part, at least, they were justified because ultimately they saved lives, both Allied and Japanese, by hastening the end of the war, even if they had a horrific toll in the cities and areas around where they fell, especially of civilians. President Obama, who was awarded the Nobel peace prize in 2009, visited Hiroshima in 2016 and saw the site where the bomb fell. President Reagan apologized in 1988 to Japanese Americans who were interned during the Second World War when he signed the Civil Liberties Act. Ten weeks after the bombing of Pearl Harbor, 120,000 Japanese-Americans and permanent residents had been made to live under guard in various camps across the United States. As a result of that Act, each surviving victim received $20,000 in reparation as well as the formal apology.

At the Lambeth Conference in 1998, the Archbishop and Bishops of the Japanese Anglican Church, the Nippon Sei Ko Kai, made a bold and deeply moving apology for not speaking out more clearly in their own country against the horrors of the Second World War. They did so on 6 August, the anniversary of the dropping of the atomic bomb on Hiroshima. It is also the date on which Christians remember, give thanks for and celebrate the transfiguration of Christ, the occasion when Jesus was at prayer and lit up by an intensity of light in front of his three closest disciples. The Japanese Archbishop said that, although the world's way may be to disfigure and scar, God's way is to transfigure and heal. Forgiveness is possible and key to that healing.

In 2006, the Archbishop of Canterbury also voiced an apology on behalf of the Church of England when, following a debate in the Church's governing body, the General Synod, he apologized for the Church's involvement in slavery. This was close to the two-hundredth anniversary of the abolition of slavery. Archbishop Rowan Williams said that the apology was necessary because we 'share the shame and the sinfulness of our predecessors', though it is not entirely clear exactly what this means.

In what way can anyone 'share the shame' of another person? We may well be affected by the shame of another and regret it, but that is not quite the same as sharing the shame itself.

If the leader of an organization or institution can legitimately voice an apology on its behalf, is it possible to voice an expression of forgiveness on behalf of an organization or nation?

The Church of England's General Synod debate with its subsequent apology and also that of the Nippon Sei Ko Kai, both raise the issue of organizations apologizing for events from many years in their past. The Japanese Anglicans were looking back well within living memory, but the English Anglicans were looking 200 years earlier.

The British Prime Minister, Tony Blair, followed the Archbishop of Canterbury's apology for the slave trade later that same year. He said:

> Personally, I believe the bicentenary offers us a chance not just to say how profoundly shameful the slave trade was – how we condemn its existence utterly and praise those who fought for its abolition, but also to express our deep sorrow that it ever happened, that it ever could have happened and to rejoice at the different and better times we live in today.

The statement did not itself apologize, though the Prime Minister did say subsequently to the Ghanaian President that 'We are sorry and I say it again'.

There are clearly many different ways in which people express sadness, regret and apology, and many different layers given to the words. For a whole mixture of reasons, some may wish to give the impression of apologizing when in fact their words do not actually say that.

In addition to words of apology, there is the question of whether or not reparation should be made, by whom, to whom, and in what form. Once more, these are far from straightforward issues, as the anti-slavery debates remind us.

Those debates also remind us that while there was a slave trade from Africa to Europe and America, there was also a slave trade to the Middle East and one within Africa itself, which had begun many years earlier. If one nation makes an apology or expresses regret in such a complex matter, then how does that relate to the involvement and lack of any apology or regret from other nations? Clearly one is not contingent upon another, but the apology and regret of one is bound to contrast with a lack of apology or regret of another.

Furthermore, how does such an expression of apology or regret for past actions connect with present-day issues of slavery, over which those apologizing are more likely to be able to have some influence? Might not an apology for the past in such circumstances appear a little hollow if it were not matched with a renewed endeavour to eliminate present-day slavery?

Is it meaningful, right and helpful to apologize for an organization or nation's involvement in slavery 200 years ago? If it is, then is it right to apologize for a war 300 years ago? Or 400? Is there a point at which we are mindful to draw a line and say this far back but no farther? How would we make such a decision? Where should the line be drawn? By whom?

Because the Church is not just a body that exists at any one time but rather across history, we are caught up in the actions of our predecessors. In a similar way, as members of society and of a nation, we are caught up to some degree with the actions of our predecessors.

For example, we may live in a flat built by a family or corporation that gained its wealth from slavery. Alternatively, most of us use roads that still follow the historic course of those built by slaves in Roman times.

The tentacles of the ancient, as well as the more recent, past spread out to the present and reach into the future. No generation begins with a clean sheet. We build society now on the shoulders, decisions and actions of those who have gone before us, whether we like it or not. Some of what we build upon will be more obviously good; other parts will be more questionable or clearly have malign strands. At the moment, for instance, the popularist view is for the British and other former colonial powers to apologize unreservedly for acts of colonialism as though everything to do with empire was bad. While no one is likely to want to try to justify abuses of power, imprisonments, slavery, sexual exploitation, stealing of resources and so on, or specific horrors such as the massacre at Amritsar and the far worse horrors that resulted from the 1947 partition of India, not everything should be seen as malign. Far from it. There are elements of the past, such as political order, relative absence of corruption, freedom of movement, legal systems, the infrastructure of roads, railways and drains, hospitals and schools, even a common language, which have brought lasting benefits. However, having a debate about such matters is extremely difficult when passions run high with opinions quickly formed and forcefully expressed. Witness the opprobrium heaped on Professor Nigel Biggar of Oxford University when he raised such issues,[4] and that at a university which surely is committed to freedom of speech, rational debate, weighing of evidence and different points of view, rather than the unthinking expression of feelings and prejudice.

Apology, remorse and reparation can clearly be a right path for more recent malign acts, but it will continue to be debatable as to how far back the trail should be taken and in what way, just as it may remain unclear quite what is the meaning or value of apologies relating to the more distant past.

One of the many complicating aspects of the ongoing debate about who might apologize for what and when is the fact that we look from the perspective of our present-day attitudes and experiences, knowledge and hindsight, and project them backwards to the time and issues in question. It is all too easy to slip into the assumption that our forebears looked with the same eyes that we do, or that they should have done, when of course we know that they did not and could not. Perspectives, interpretations, value systems, attitudes, knowledge, understanding, social mores, and so much more, continue to evolve and change, we hope for the better, though even that may be more questionable than we care to admit.

As a result, apologizing for past events can be done without fully appreciating how people thought about and approached the issues now occasioning the apology. The question needs to be asked whether, had we actually been there and been subject to the same social context and values, we might not have done exactly what they did. How much of our own present judgement do we take with us when we try to look through someone else's eyes in the past? Is our apology saying that, living at that time in our history, those who took a decision we now regard as mistaken or wrong should have known better and decided differently, or are we saying that we, with our hindsight, current value systems and attitudes, look at what they did and, projecting our views backwards, regard the decision as mistaken and wrong? The apology means something slightly different in each case.

Our apologies for the past can be a bit like the kind of historical drama which seems to amount to little more than contemporary characters acting in an eighteenth-century story with matching costume but taking their twenty-first-century questions and attitudes with them. It lacks authenticity and realism and so weakens both its plot and message. If this is to be avoided, then we must work really hard to enter the mindset of our forebears whose judgement we are now rejecting, otherwise the apology becomes cheapened and shallow. This is always going to be difficult to achieve, if not impossible. Perhaps we should accept that any apparent apology for the historical past is essentially a statement of deep regret that something happened, with an acknowledgement that, with our present perspective, values and attitudes, it is a course of action that we now regard as wrong and wish had never taken place.

Just as it is a vexed issue as to whether it is right for nations and institutions to apologize for events long in the past, so it is also problematic as to what it would then mean for the ones apologizing, if they were to be forgiven, since it was not they who caused the offences. It is also problematic because of the difficulty of knowing what did or did not actually happen and of identifying the chain reaction that then flowed. Some strands may be clear, others broken or lost. Even for recent events involving ourselves, our memory may not be as reliable as we like to think. Older events involving many others from years before are never going to be fully clear.

We all have a tendency, when recalling what has happened to us, to do a certain amount of reconstruction in order to make ourselves out better in some regard than we really were, to tell the story to our own advantage. Even if at the first telling the story is only minutely changed, when the second telling comes along, which version do we remember? Perhaps the recounted and reconstructed story replaces the first memory, or at least becomes entwined with it. If the story is retold many times, then at the very least it is likely to have drifted a little, perhaps a lot, and may have become highly embellished. We may think still that it is our memory, and so in a manner it is, but now it is the memory of our own recounting as well as our memory of the original event, with the two entangled in some ill-defined and unknowable way.

Memories drift and change. They are not quite the fixed realities we mostly imagine them to be. Even at the outset they are selective and can be very unreliable. Witnesses of a road accident can give different colours for the cars involved, different accounts of how the people were dressed, the speed of the vehicles, and so on. All these people will be sure that they are being accurate in their evidence as they recall it. With time, the recall can be even less reliable. A story does not need much retelling, either to others or to ourselves, before it is likely to have changed.

It is not that we set out deliberately to reconstruct the past, but rather that the drift creeps up on us and skews what we remember or think we remember.

Sometimes, in cases of extreme horror, we will choose not to remember because of the revulsion and hurt involved. We do not want even to look at the experience again or be reminded of it. In such cases, whether we like it or not, the experience may be so deeply etched within us that even without any revisiting of what happened, it will be crystal clear. Sometimes, however, precisely because of the pain, we reconstruct and amend the memory so that it causes less new hurt than would the real memory.

We cannot forgive what we refuse to remember, and it is not straightforward to forgive what we have altered or distorted in our memory because we no longer know reliably what it is that needs forgiving.

There are cultures which encourage remembering, just as there are ones which encourage forgetfulness. Which dominates is likely to depend upon what the cultural attitude is towards what is disclosed. If an organization purports to welcome whistle-blowing, for example, but in practice ensures that the whistle-blowers are never promoted, or are dismissed, then it will not be surprising if employees are encouraged to forget, or at least not voice their memories and perceptions of injustice and wrongdoing. It is too easy for whistle-blowers to be accused of disloyalty, betraying confidences, instigating trouble or damaging the team if a culture of blame or wilful subversion of the truth is dominant. But if an organization has a culture where there is a genuine desire to acknowledge injustice, then there will be encouragement for people to remember and speak out.

In his book, *Black Box Thinking*, Matthew Syed draws attention to aspects of this in terms of the need to acknowledge failure, learn from it and change. He recognizes that blame is entirely counter-productive as it drives down the number of failures and mistakes that are reported, so reducing the opportunities to learn and improve. His book's title refers to what might be regarded as the technical remembering of the black box in every aircraft, the data from which enables the industry to improve performance and safety. This would not be possible if a blame culture dominated.

Syed refers as well to the success of the Mercedes F1 team with its readiness to acknowledge failure and its willingness to engage with it positively so that improvements could always be introduced.

By contrast, the health service and police force seem to struggle more to acknowledge mistakes and learn from them, perhaps because of the influence of a culture of blame and the fear of litigation.

If the focus is on best possible performance and outcomes, then awareness of mistakes and failings will always be essential for future learning. That means that an organization must hold in tension the striving after the best possible performance with the acceptance that, at times, mistakes will be made and need to be admitted. If the pursuit of excellence is too dominant, then it is hard to admit to anything that is less than perfect, but if the culture errs the other way, so that it is thought to be too accepting of failure and mistakes, then the motivation to produce the best will be weakened. The right balance in this tension is not far from acceptance and forgiveness when they are properly understood.

The Christian life is about this very tension of aspiring to the best but being forgiven for mistakes along the way. Jesus challenges his disciples at one point – 'Be perfect'[5] – but is always there to forgive, encourage, heal and inspire.

When a bishop saw his clergy privately, he would ask them what they had failed at recently and what had not gone well. His intention was not to apportion blame; quite the opposite. He recognized that if the clergy were trying new ways of exercising their ministry and mission and leading their congregations creatively, then some of the new ventures might work while others would not. If there were no failures, there were likely to be no successes either. There would also be less that was new, less openness, less growth and learning, both personally and ministerially. Fear of failure and undue caution can stifle, just as recklessness can destroy. Deliberately asking about failure was a way of trying to reduce the fear of it and so encourage experimentation and newness. He was signifying that it was not only all right to fail but bound to happen if new ideas were being explored. Naturally enough, having asked about failures, the bishop went on to ask about the successes too.

If we live in a culture of acceptance, affirmation and forgiveness, and especially if we were brought up with those qualities, we are more likely to be able to forgive because we have learnt from an early stage what it is to be forgiven. Like reservoirs or canals, we can only pass on what we receive. If the way of forgiveness has not flowed into us, it is very difficult for it to flow out.

There are some who find it much harder to forgive. If what has been modelled to us is to hold on to grudges and resentments, it is small wonder if that is what we practise. Learning to forgive with this background is doubly hard: old patterns must be set aside and a new way found.

It is also harder to forgive when an offence brings to mind some earlier and greater offence done to us. Echoes from our own past and memories of previous hurts make forgiving far more difficult. It is harder too if we have forgiven a person for saying or doing something that they later repeat. We ask ourselves whether they really meant it when they said 'Sorry'. How can we know whether or not they mean it this time? Should we forgive them anyway, or is that simply going to encourage them to do it yet again?

I can recall an engaged couple in a group preparing for marriage, which my wife and I were leading some years ago. We asked them at one point on the course to tell each other something that the other one said which they particularly valued. We then asked them to tell each other something they found difficult or upsetting.

The next morning, there was a ring on our doorbell at the vicarage. A woman was standing there, clearly very upset. She was a stranger to me, but I invited her in and she immediately said, 'I don't know what you said to them last night, but they have decided not to get married!' It wasn't difficult to ascertain that she was the mother of Anne who was engaged to Julian, or at least had been the previous evening when they came to our marriage preparation group. I asked Anne's mother whether the decision was a good thing or a bad thing. Her reaction was interesting. Initially she appeared to be even more cross, and then she seemed to reflect on the question. She had the grace to say, 'Do you know, I am not sure.' That enabled us to talk more about it all, and for my wife and me to see Anne and Julian that evening.

It transpired that when Anne was asked to share something that her fiancé said which she did not like, she told Julian that it really irritated her when she came home in the evening and he always asked her, 'Where have you been?' Apparently, this was precisely what her father used to ask when she was a teenager, and in the same tone of voice. She had not come to terms with it then, and Julian now was inadvertently pressing the same sore spot in her memory. They had a terrible row on their way home, which led to calling off the wedding. Thankfully, they were able not only to talk more about it but also to understand what was happening and why, so that they could forgive one another. Anne also forgave her father, and was the stronger for it. The wedding went ahead as planned.

We all are likely to have some 'sore spots' from our pasts and we need to be aware that if others touch them or tread on them then we may overreact. The memory and experience can still hurt because we have not yet fully resolved the issue or perhaps fully forgiven the person who hurt us. The sore is not yet healed.

The famous passage of St Paul to the Christians in Corinth about love has in it the phrase, 'Love keeps no score of wrongs.'[6] Yet it is surprisingly easy for us not only to remember wrongs done to us but to count them, sometimes deliberately, so as to throw them back at the other party next time there is an argument. There are some who, when faced with a challenge in a relationship, ask for evidence of alleged misdemeanours, demanding, 'Where's your evidence? Give me an example.' They effectively ask the other person to count and wilfully remember past wrongs rather than forgive and let go of them. Such a way of relating and arguing builds in seeds of destruction. If no 'evidence' is forthcoming, then the one asking for it feels triumphant, and if it is remembered and fired back, the one recalling it feels either victorious or else pained at having to keep this score of wrongs and defend themselves. Either way, both lose, and the relationship is harmed.

There was a woman whose child was injured in a road accident. The child was in hospital for weeks before being sufficiently well to return home. Even then, her parents knew that she would never fully recover. The mother was totally exhausted with the worry and the continual hospital visiting, while still caring for the rest of the family and trying to hold down her job. She felt that the anger she harboured against the driver, although it stopped her from sleeping properly at night, gave her the energy to get through the days. Her friends saw that the anger was increasingly taking over and changing who she was. It had become all-consuming. It was not only her motivation for all that she had to do each day but also beginning to drown out her underlying love and care. She suffered from severe headaches and insomnia, for which she had to be on daily medication, but she seemed unaware of the connection between that and the anger in her heart.

Being able to forgive is one thing, but finding the way to do so can be quite different and is always a lifetime's work.

4

Offering forgiveness

Faced with violence of any kind done to us or those whom we love, it might be thought amazing that forgiveness ever comes to be offered at all. As those who have been in this situation best know, the path is likely to be immensely painful and slow, with setbacks along the way. The path of each person, even those facing similar horrors, will be different, perhaps very different.

A father of two teenagers was walking along the pavement when he was knocked down and killed by a hit-and-run driver who was never caught. His wife could not come to terms with what had happened and felt a horrendous, paralysing emptiness. Their teenage son lashed out at those around him as he sought to cope with what had happened, while his younger sister kept thinking every day that her father would still walk through the door, call her name and give her a longed-for hug. Each struggled with a different aspect of grief:[1] the man's wife was in a state of shock, their son in anger and their daughter in denial. Each had the same nightmare to contend with, but in their own way, separate from one another. Each had to work through what they were experiencing and at their own speed. Each needed others to listen to them and encourage them to go back over what had happened and was happening, retelling their experience again and again in their own words as, slowly, they came through to more acceptance.

All who work with those who have suffered tragedy will attest to how vital it is that people are not only free to tell their story, but also able to retell it again and again, without others becoming impatient or interrupting and certainly not telling them to move on or get over it. Each time it is told, it becomes possible to accept a little more of what has happened, and to do so a little more deeply and with a little bit more of oneself. Each recounting can help with this process of acceptance, especially in the early days, even though that may be the last thing which the person thinks they really want to happen. The inner scream may not be heard by others but is all too real and loud.

Some of this can also apply to a person who has inflicted harm. They might be thinking, 'How could I have done such a thing? I can never live with myself again.' They also need listening to and help to come to terms with what they have done, with their inner scream and shout being expressed and heard.

Terry Waite, a previous Archbishop of Canterbury's Special Envoy in the Middle East, was taken hostage as he sought to secure the release of hostages in Beirut. He was held a prisoner for nearly five years, the first four of which were in solitary confinement.

After his release, Terry Waite wrote a book about his experiences, *Taken on Trust*. He later said in an interview, that writing the book

> over a period of about 12 months was a therapeutic exercise. It enabled me to objectify the experience. As you objectify it, you come to terms with it, rather than it coming to terms with you inwardly ... If you can understand why people behave as they behave, at least you can be on the road to forgiveness.[2]

Years later, Terry Waite was able to go back to Beirut and meet his captors and so further the journey of forgiving them.

What Terry Waite speaks of as 'objectifying the experience' comes about for most people by telling the story. In this case it came about by telling it in a book as well as speaking about it to others. In the process of that telling, the experience becomes, at one level, an object, something out there rather than just inside us. Of course, what is 'out there' is in many respects very different from what is inside the person, but it is recognizably the same experience. Being able to begin to hear and see it changes it. As Terry Waite said, the process is very slow. Yet, it begins. Like everything else, it too is a journey.

For this to happen, there must be at least one good listener who listens but also encourages the telling – not just once but many times. Listening is both a gift and a skill that must be learnt and developed. We all need to be heard and understood, especially when we have been wronged or hurt.

Receiving good listening is one of the ways in which those suffering most from horrors or trauma can begin to come to terms with what has happened and risk embarking on their journey of forgiveness. As a fellow human being, the listener can recognize and even, if only slightly, relate to some elements of the unique story and pain about which they are hearing, though its depth and scale may be way beyond what most people can begin to imagine let alone experience.

The art of listening is crucial. It is not, however, as straightforward as it may seem, neither as a skill nor with the issues that it raises. Very often those who have suffered trauma or abuse blame themselves to some degree when it may well not be their fault at all. Victims are likely to need reassurance and acceptance, as well as knowing that it is safe for them to speak, that they are not about to be blamed. They need focused attention and understanding from their listener, with space and lack of interruption in a safe space, so that they can tell their story.

Many pastoral training courses will focus a good deal on how to listen, and rightly so. It is a way of reaching out to the other person, giving them undivided attention, expressing how much they matter in themselves, as the person they are. Good listening affirms us and tells us that we are of value and worth. It also says that it is safe to speak about a horror, to risk articulating it, that it will not be ignored or laughed at, belittled or denied, dismissed or judged, but heard with utmost seriousness. If listening is a gift, so is receiving a confidence, especially if you are the first person to be trusted with this secret.

Training programmes that are offered to help people respond to disclosures of abuse will usually tell those hearing a disclosure always to believe what they hear. There is a vital truth behind this requirement, namely that of affirming and encouraging the victim who is risking speaking, perhaps for the first time, so that they have the confidence to tell their story and be heard, knowing that they are safe in doing so. If a victim summons up the courage to speak openly for the first time about some past horror, they need to be believed, otherwise they will feel like withdrawing once more, shrivelling up, never to risk speaking again, and so the abuse, about which they are risking speaking, is compounded. Fear of not being believed is a strong motivating force in not disclosing.

It is not for a person first listening to a disclosure of abuse or trauma to make a judgement about the veracity of what they are hearing, except maybe in very exceptional circumstances if it is obvious that the story is malicious, or if the person listening is a social worker or police officer who has additional information. A listener may need at some points to ask questions to encourage and to clarify, but not at first hearing to challenge or express doubt about the underlying facts. At a later stage it may be necessary for one of the professionals involved to do so, especially if there is any question of further action, for example as part of a criminal investigation, if that is what results, but the first listening and befriending is about encouraging the telling of the story and reassuring the victim. Good listening inevitably means entering into something of the pain that the victim is sharing. We cannot, as fellow human beings, be unmoved by what we hear. If it is costly to listen, it is immensely costlier to speak.

Conveying to someone disclosing abuse, trauma or violence that their story is taken seriously has a significant bearing on how we also act on the crucial truth that the person against whom the allegations are being made is, in the eyes of the law and more generally, to be regarded as innocent until they are proved guilty. There is a danger in our culture at present of reversing this principle in the case of allegations of rape or other abuse. Abuse, especially child abuse, has become regarded as unforgivable by some, with vilification and blame gratuitously extended and expressed in the media as soon as an allegation is made and a person named. Harm is done to innocent people if false allegations are brought against them. There are too many stories, including those of high-profile individuals, who have been accused but then had their cases dropped, though usually with the characteristic Crown Prosecution Service language of 'insufficient evidence'. We have not found a way of stopping thrown mud from sticking, nor of saying that someone is indeed innocent when cases collapse. If we were more robust and consistent about maintaining a person's innocence until it was proved otherwise, we might be readier to see the collapse of a case as a reaffirmation of innocence.

We have not yet found a way as a society to balance the need on the one hand of encouraging victims to come forward and on the other of not causing irreparable damage to a person's reputation and life when allegations are shown to be untrue. We must ensure that those who risk speaking out are trusted and encouraged to do so safely, but we also have to ensure that we find a way of restating again and again that presumed innocence continues to cover all cases and situations, including ones of alleged abuse.

A tragic case of false allegations was brought against a teacher who was accused of inappropriately touching some female pupils. It later transpired that he was innocent of the charge, and indeed, not even in the relevant building at the time alleged. Nevertheless, he was suspended during the police enquiry, and the young boy that he and his wife had only recently adopted was removed from their care, never to be returned, even when the allegations were shown to be false. The teacher in question was also restricted from spending time alone with his own teenage son. False accusations do irreparable harm to those wrongly accused and to their families, very often with lifelong consequences.

There needs to be a very strong presumption that when allegations are shown to be false, as opposed to not proven, then the complainant will be prosecuted with real rigour.

Another aspect of the difficulties involved for our social services and police is knowing when and how to probe the narrative that a victim of abuse is describing without conveying the impression that they are not being believed. There is also the question of what language is used subsequently to refer to the person. Should they be spoken of as a 'victim' or 'alleged victim' or 'complainant'? The Independent Inquiry into Child Sexual Abuse (IICSA) is said currently to be favouring referring to those who have told their story of abuse as 'complainants'. Speaking of them as 'victims' might be thought to imply that a judgement has already been reached, prematurely, about the veracity of what they are saying, which would threaten to undermine police impartiality and could be thought, in some cases, to contribute to miscarriages of justice. However, victims of abuse of any kind need to be believed and trusted for what they are reporting and that very process is part of their journey of healing. If they are listened to in an atmosphere that is not one of trusting and believing, they will hear suspicion and doubt, which will cause them further harm.

The central issue is a clash between the pastoral need of one party with the impartial fairness due to the other party and the legal process. These pull in different directions. Perhaps a way forward is to distinguish the pastoral from the legal, so as to ensure that legal officers themselves can remain true to their obligation to be impartial and unbiased in their gathering of evidence, and not be put into the situation of being the first person to whom victims speak. It would be possible for the police to have trained pastoral carers and listeners to be with victims for initial meetings. The Independent Inquiry into Child Sexual Abuse (IICSA) currently does this with its Truth Project and now has some experience which could be drawn upon. It would then be possible for the proper probing of a complainant's testimony to take place subsequently in order to ensure, as far as is possible, that the allegation is not false.

It is clear that this vexed and painful issue needs better resolution than it has currently. As it stands, the process is skewed: in most cases there is little redress against, and few consequences for, or prosecutions of, those who bring wrong or even deliberately false or malicious accusations, whereas there are immense, irreversible and often life-changing consequences for those wrongly accused. It also needs remembering that the total number of false allegations is a very small proportion of the cases dealt with, but the category still exists and so does the need to resolve its issues.

Lesley Bilinda has written very movingly about forgiving those who killed her Rwandan husband, Charles, in the genocide of 1994.[3] At the time, she had been running a community health programme with Tearfund, and her husband was Archdeacon of the area. In April 1994, she left their home in Gahini for a short holiday with her sister in Kenya. It was while she was away that Charles was abducted and presumed killed, though no one knew for sure. Being away when the horror happened was later to add to Lesley's sense of guilt, a feeling commonly shared by those in similar situations.

It was a long time before she could become certain as to her husband's fate, even though his death seemed all too likely from the beginning. Because it would have been so unsafe for her to return from Kenya to the village in Rwanda where she had been living for five years, she returned instead to her native Scotland, where from that distance she tried to find out as much as she could about what had happened. With no news from Charles himself, and increasingly bad news from so many others, it became progressively clear what his fate must have been. Even so, it was six agonizing months before her worst fears were indeed confirmed by Charles's sister who, remarkably, had survived the slaughter.

Ten years after the murder of her husband, Lesley Bilinda was able to return to Rwanda. During that visit she met two of those imprisoned for crimes of genocide, who it was thought might have been involved directly in Charles being killed, though both denied it.

She wrote:

> I thought long and hard about forgiving those who had been responsible for murdering him. Was it possible to forgive someone without knowing who they were? And if I had never met them or even seen them and they were thousands of miles away, would it mean anything anyway? But I felt I had to try to forgive, for my sake if nothing else. Deep inside I was very angry and bitter over what had happened, and I knew that in time, if unchecked, this bitterness could destroy me.[4]

It is this honesty and insight which helped enable Lesley to move towards forgiving. For anyone who has suffered great pain and hurt, or indeed lesser ones, forgiveness cannot begin to be offered to those responsible without first facing up to something of the pain and hurt being suffered, as well as any anger and guilt, bitterness and resentment, that may be present.

Lesley Bilinda wrote subsequently of four choices that she had to make to walk this path of forgiveness, beginning with

> the need to acknowledge the reality and horror of what has happened and to own the strength of our feelings in response.

Trying to deny or forget our anger and pain will not diminish them but rather suppress them, storing them up inside to surface again at some later date – even years later – at a time we least expect it. It is far better to be honest about the strength of our feelings.

She goes on to say:

However, acknowledging such feelings towards those who have wronged us does not mean we need to act on those feelings. Much as I might want to retaliate and cause suffering in return, I need to recognize that taking such action will benefit no one. So my second choice is not to take action to revenge or retaliate for what has been done to me.[5]

This is common to all victims of great violence. Acknowledging the reality of the pain is doubly difficult because it is both a struggle to be honest about it as well as desperately painful to recall it. But the need to do so is crucial if there is to be a beginning of the journey of forgiveness. Where the pain remains buried, denied, unacknowledged and unrecognized, the journey cannot properly start. This is not to say that the anguish must be fully acknowledged before any beginning can be made because the acknowledging itself is also a journey. It is enough, in order to begin, to face up to only a very little, knowing that there is much more that lies buried and that can be addressed at some later stage. If we had to face up to all of it at once, it would be overwhelming.

Furthermore, as Lesley Bilinda discovered when she returned to Rwanda ten years after her husband's murder, the issues involved are often far more complicated than they seem at first sight. She had to face not only her grief at her husband's murder but also the emotions that came to the surface while meeting so many people who were in the area at the time, including a witness to the brutal murder of a great friend, and those who told her of her husband's unfaithfulness. This great seething of very mixed emotions, experiences and memories made her realize that it was not only a question of learning to forgive but there was also some element of needing to be forgiven.

Archbishop Desmond Tutu has written, with his daughter Mpho, about this same theme of beginning to forgive.[6] They too offer four stages of the path that they discern, albeit different ones from Lesley Bilinda, but, like her, recognize how vital it is to 'name the hurt' and face our feelings.

John Monbourquette, in his book *How to Forgive*,[7] identified 12 steps of what he called 'true forgiveness', and, like Lesley Bilinda and the Tutus, began with the need not to seek revenge and also to recognize one's pain and poverty. These have been recurring themes in the experiences and writings of those who have begun to come to terms with great suffering and those who have been able to assist them in the process.

Facing the pain is not made any easier in our Western cultures by the extent and lengths to which we go, at so many different levels and in such diverse ways, to avoid pain altogether. Obviously, no one wants to be in pain, and severe pain threatens to be all-consuming for those who have to endure it. Yet there are aspects of pain that are necessary, even if we seem predisposed not to recognize the fact.

If we put our hand accidentally over a flame, then pain tells us instantly to move it. If a child steals money from his or her mother's purse, then that child is likely to have a guilty conscience which will cause a different kind of pain, but again it is pain which says, 'Do something about it: put it right.'

Pain is not all bad, nor should all pain be avoided. I was speaking recently to someone whose husband had died not long before. Her GP had told her that she was suffering from post-traumatic stress disorder and needed medication. That may have been so, but her pain and distress were natural parts of grief and loss. While it may be helpful to those who grieve to be prescribed medication, especially when sleep seems impossible, our cultural avoidance of pain may ultimately slow down the process of grieving. How can there not be pain at the loss of a close friend, spouse or partner? If there has been joy at being together, is there not bound to be sorrow at being apart? The deeper the joy, the greater the sorrow is likely to be. In any very close friendship, partnership or marriage, one of the two involved is likely to die before the other, who then has to bear the grief and its pain on behalf of the two of them.

There can be similar issues about the bearing of pain for those who are dying, and for their relatives and doctors. Thankfully, the whole development of palliative care has made it possible for most to die without the extremes of pain which those in previous generations had to suffer. However, questions must still be faced about the levels and timings of drugs to be administered so that patients are neither in the nightmare of unendurable pain nor the oblivion of drug-induced unconsciousness. What is manageable for one person will be different for another, as people's pain endurance and thresholds vary so widely. Different people will choose to endure different levels of pain for the sake of being conscious throughout a stage of illness. There is no right or wrong choice: each person must decide for themselves. However, pain itself is unlikely to be completely avoidable and, even if it were, the avoidance may be thought to come at too high a price.

It was fashionable to refer to death as 'the great unmentionable', and, for some, pain has joined the same category. With such attitudes growing in prevalence, facing up to pain is made harder. Yet it is vital to do so, which means that those coping with the pain and hurt of some great wrong done to them have to be counter-cultural at more than one level.

It is not just society's attitude to avoiding pain which must be overcome by those who would walk the path and way of forgiveness. There are many other obstacles that can lie along the journey or try to stop it even beginning. We have already referred to the Tutsi woman who felt so guilty at not forgiving that she thought that there could be no forgiveness for her. This has been paralleled many times for me as I have listened to people who have been abused in childhood and feel guilty in adult life that they cannot forgive. Then, of course, they feel guilty at feeling guilty, which makes everything even worse and compounds the abuse.

In such encounters, I have asked the victim of abuse if they want to forgive their abuser. Very often the reply was negative. In which case, I would ask, 'Do you *want to want* to forgive?' This question often prompted a thoughtful silence before the person would be able to say that they did *want to want* to forgive. I was then able to say that they were already on the way, that they had begun their journey of forgiveness.

Deep down in us is the desire not to be burdened by guilt, but rather for our innate goodness to rise up and overcome evil and everything that opposes that goodness. However, trauma and extreme experiences of horror create an enormous barrier so that it seems impossible to even begin the process of dismantling it or knowing how to surmount it. Yet our innate goodness and desire to see right prevail provide an energy and motivation not to give up but to keep hope alive. We still want there to be a way out, a way to forgive, even in the face of an apparently unscalable barrier, so that we are not overcome but can breathe and live again more fully and freely. 'Wanting to want' can provide the start of the route, the road, the bridge, the beginning of the way over and through the barrier so that goodness is not overcome but can start to grow once more.

The attitude that you either forgive or don't forgive is held far too widely in society and is itself a major obstacle to forgiving. It is also not true. Forgiveness, like the spiritual realities of love, hope and faith, is a journey. It almost never happens instantly. It is a process.

No one can tell how far along the journey of forgiveness the victim of some terrible abuse or other trauma may travel in their lifetime, but what is important is that they begin. Wanting to want to forgive makes a start. The fact that they are moving, and going in the right direction, is far more important than the speed of travel or exactly how far along the journey they have gone. Those issues will mostly take care of themselves.

In these situations, if we are to keep moving, then there are likely to be other serious obstacles to overcome along the way. One of these will be the difference between our head and our heart. It is, as we have recognized already, out of our wills that forgiveness comes initially, which is why the title of the book by Antoine Leiris, *You Will Not Have My Hate*, is so brilliant. He did not choose for a title, 'I don't want you to have my hate' nor 'I hope you won't have my hate', but 'You will not have'. There is here deliberate choice, conviction, will. Antoine Leiris wrote out of the pain and tragedy of discovering that his wife Hélène had been killed by terrorists, along with 88 other victims, at the Bataclan Theatre in Paris on 13 November 2015. Like the relatives and friends of all the others murdered that day, he had to struggle not just with the anguish of being devastated by grief but the pull of his head against the agony of his heart.

While our head can choose to begin the journey of forgiving, that does not mean that our heart has reached the same place and is also ready to begin. We can say 'Yes' to forgiving with our heads while still wanting to shout 'No' with our hearts, because it all hurts too much. However, having begun the journey with the head, the heart is encouraged, even helped, in facing up to the hurts and coming to terms with them more and more.

In the Old Testament book of Ezekiel, there is a powerful image used about hearts of stone and hearts of flesh.[8] It is associated with God's promise of forgiveness, of making clean with water and making new, of taking out the heart of stone and replacing it with a heart of flesh. We refer to the same image when we speak of someone being 'hard-hearted' or 'cold-hearted'. Hearts of stone remain hard, cold, unchanging and unmovable. Hearts of flesh will hurt more but can also live and be warm, throb and love.

If we decline to say with our wills and minds that others will not have our hate, then we make it more likely that our hearts stay cold, even frozen, hard with the hurts and pains, numb and frigid. If we risk beginning to at least want to want to forgive, then our heart of stone can be replaced by a living heart of flesh once more, which can pulse and become warmed again. Such a journey opens us to the pain of the heart, but also to its hope, its life, its possibilities and potential.

There are other obstacles to the journey of forgiveness not unrelated to the pain of the heart. When the trauma that is being recalled is just too much with which to cope, perhaps because of other issues and events going on at the same time in other parts of our lives, then even when there is a will to cope there may not be a way or the necessary energy at that stage. Perhaps the other issues and events need some level of resolution first, before there is sufficient energy available once more to look again at the anguish and begin the healing.

The replaying of trauma of an experience is likely to be expressed in our dreams. Recurrent nightmares are common among victims of extreme experiences. Eric Lomax, who wrote the *Railway Man*, suffered from the same horrendous nightmare many times each night, every night of his life for over 50 years. It came as a consequence of the torture to which he was subjected as a Far Eastern Prisoner of War (FEPOW) under the Japanese when he was captured at the fall of Singapore in 1942. Such experiences can overwhelm people's lives, dominating each day and certainly each night.

Another obstacle to offering forgiveness results from the way in which we can grow 'familiar' even with horrendous situations in which we find ourselves. Because coming to terms with what has happened is such a difficult and protracted process, past experiences inevitably continue to shape parts of our development and outlook during that time, even if their power over us is waning. If the horror has subjected us in some form or other to being a victim of abuse of any kind, as part of our recovery we will have to learn to come out of the victim mode that has been thrust upon us by an abuse of power. While that may be what we yearn to happen, it can take time and effort and be less straightforward than we might expect. During the process, we are likely to find ourselves with a transition taking place, out of victim mode into the recovery of our full personhood, with its sense of independence, freedom and responsibility. For a stage, these qualities, which we had taken for granted previously, might surprise us in being unfamiliar, and can be so to a point where they are difficult, even seeming, temporarily, to be unknown. If this happens, despite all that we wish for, something of the familiarity of our previous situation can be what we find ourselves holding on to, precisely because it is familiar and, for the moment, easier; it does not require us to make the effort to walk into what is now surprisingly unknown. Those who have been in anything like this situation will be aware that refusing to let oneself be defined as a victim is an exhausting 24/7 task.

Another associated danger of this victimhood is that it is quite likely to affect how others relate to us. If we receive a level of attention and care that is different to what we experienced before, then we may, however much we hate the victimhood itself, feel ambivalent to some of its consequences. This can be very difficult to cope with. The last thing we may be likely to want is for any good to come to us as a result of the evil of the ordeal, and it can catch us off guard if that appears to be happening, especially if we find ourselves referring to the victimhood in order to receive empathy or similar positive responses and attention from others.

Holding on to victimhood is not something that anyone is likely to want to do deliberately and consciously, but it can influence behaviour in unexpected ways, including the speed of transition and recovery from the horrors to which we have been subjected. As people recover from their experiences, so they are able once more to see their identity as valued and loved, responsible, free adults who might have been victims once but definitely are no longer. As victims, they were objects: now, once again, they are subjects. As victims, they were done to, but now are free to choose what they do. As victims, they were deperson-alized, but now have personhood restored. As victims, they were rubbished, but now have dignity restored. As victims, others exercised power over them, but now they have their own power returned. The experience and the victimhood are part of their past, a past which has clearly shaped who they are but out of which they have grown.

Many, probably most, of those who have been victims of abuse will not only speak of themselves, but also want others to speak of them, as *survivors*. Their horror was so all-encompassing that any other language does not begin to express the enormity of what happened nor its lasting impact and entrapment. Those who have not suffered will want to respect their wishes and use of language in anything they say. However, there are others, who are survivors, who seem to reach a point in their lives when they continue to acknowledge that they are indeed survivors and asso-ciate with the term, but no longer wish that, or the language of victim, to be seen as the determinative descriptions of their past, and would prefer other vocabulary to be used for them now, per-haps that of having been a victim but one no longer because they have found a way to be free. There is a constant need to recognize and be sensitive to the fact that people use the terms of victim and survivor differently from one another, and differently at different stages in their lives. In addition, it is vital for others not to picture a relationship as being in some way imbalanced because the other person has been a victim, since this is to fail to treat the other as an equal and so push them back into victimhood.

These issues are as far from straightforward or simple as one can get; victims all have their own stories and stages, subsequent experiences and views, different intensity of emotion. What may be a helpful language or description for one person may be anathema to another and seem like a betrayal of the ongoing reality of their own pain. Each person's journey is unique, and language reflects this.

Just as individuals vary greatly in how they want to speak about both their experiences and also themselves in the light of those experiences, so it also needs acknowledging that the actual harm done varies hugely from one incident to another. There is a vast range of abuse. The most extreme experiences are horrendous but there are also lesser forms and some relatively minor ones which are still nevertheless abusive. Less extreme acts may cause considerably less trauma, though what is 'less extreme' for one person may be extremely grave to another. Just as people's physical pain thresholds vary enormously, so do their emotional pain thresholds and responses. One person is able to recover from an experience that another person might find far more damaging. This, too, has a significant bearing on how people use the language of victim and survivor.

There is a helpful paragraph about this issue in the Church of England's document, *Responding Well to Those who have been Sexually Abused*:

> The language employed to describe those who have suffered sexual abuse is always a sensitive matter. Few would want to be defined by an experience or experiences from their past. However, they have been *victims* and that fact must not be lost in concern about correct language. At the same time, many have moved on as far as they are able and would be better described as survivors of sexual abuse or even thrivers beyond abuse: they do not want an episode or series of episodes to be regarded as the defining moment of their lives and of who they are, however much it has dramatically and tragically influenced and shaped their lives. As far as possible in this document we have used 'those who have suffered/been the victim of sexual abuse', but the term 'survivor' is also used in an attempt to capture the complexity of the issue.[9]

Viktor Frankl had pertinent comments to make about this in his book, *Man's Search for Meaning*. He survived the concentration camp of Auschwitz but when everyone in the camp was liberated he was faced with how to survive the new and unexpected freedom. He describes how keeping alive a sense of hope and exercising an ongoing freedom of choice, in so far as it was possible, had been vital to survival in the camp itself and helped people through their horrendous ordeal of having everything stripped away and being deliberately depersonalized. The new situation of freedom was not something that it was possible to come to terms with at all quickly. He charts a path of depersonalized survivors having to avoid an equivalent of 'the bends' of deep-sea divers as they come out of one world into another, but also how they then have to cope with the lack of understanding of those around them, as well as the nightmares that had been inflicted on them. Furthermore, the hopes that had helped sustain people in the camp, including Viktor Frankl himself, might prove empty if those they longed to see again had not survived. The nightmare and suffering do not stop, but the new freedom must be lived, the stolen identity recovered, dignity restored.

The depersonalization of victimhood, the sense of being an object, being done to and used, having dignity, worth, individuality and character stripped away by others, are experiences with which all too many can relate. They are experiences that not only need overcoming but healing, so that there can be again a delight and valuing, brightness and hope, freedom and choice, liberation and responsibility, a thriving future after abuse, not just a surviving.

Whatever our route along the journey of forgiveness, then, if we are to keep moving, we shall know that it is, as Antoine Leiris[10] and others bear testimony, a daily struggle. It is bound to be like that, not only because each day is new and different, but because we inevitably find ourselves recalling and revisiting the pains and hurts and other deep emotions and issues with which we are struggling and were struggling the previous day and, quite likely, night too. These are never matters that can be resolved once for all time. We need longer, perhaps our whole life, and this means that we have not only to commit to the journey, but to recommit again and again, daily in the early stages, until the forgiving way becomes the inhabited way for us.

It ought not to surprise us that forgiveness is a daily struggle because this is true of all spiritual truths and journeys, which is partly why religions teach a pattern of daily prayer which renews people in the stream of God's love and strength. Without that daily recommitting and struggling, other paths and approaches can insinuate and distract. A spiritual path of any kind needs focus and renewal, and this includes, within the spectrum of the spiritual, the journey of forgiveness, as it does the way of love or faith or hope. Many married couples, for example, will testify that they try to ensure that they tell each other every day that they love one another. Such expressions renew and enable their way of love to continue to grow and flourish. Daily patterns strengthen us. Daily recommitments renew us. Where there are other forces at work, both within us and outside us, then an awareness of the possible need for a daily renewal becomes all the more significant, as those struggling to forgive, rather than succumb to a sense of revenge, know all too well.

Timing is an issue in other ways, too, in our journey for forgiveness. There have been some remarkable public statements of forgiveness by individuals and groups following immediately upon the murder of close relatives. At one level, these testimonies have been inspiring and an amazing example, yet in other ways have caused concern for those speaking out, lest they should retrospectively feel that they had done so too quickly, leaving them with a greater inner conflict of seeking to resolve head and heart, as well as something which they are far from sure that they can live up to. Perhaps their statements need to be understood more as a commitment to the journey than implying that total forgiveness has been achieved from the beginning.

It is always going to take time for any of us for the pain and reality of a death to impact fully, and until it does we do not really know what it is with which we shall then have to struggle to come to terms. This is all the more the case when the death has been caused by murder or terrorism. Inner journeys and developments need their own pace and space for each of us. Trying to force them prematurely can be harmful. Nevertheless, stating publicly our resolve and commitment to forgive, as Gordon

Wilson so memorably did when his daughter Marie was killed in the Enniskillen bombing, can be a means of aiding our struggle by giving us something to which to live up to and reminding us of the goal. For some, this might be helpful and be a resource to draw upon in their daily struggle to forgive, though for others it will certainly make the struggle more difficult and might even become problematic in the future.

A group of incest offenders in a treatment programme made a powerful plea about another aspect of the timing of statements of forgiveness when they said, together: 'Don't forgive us so easily.' All were Christians and had gone to their pastors as soon as they were arrested, asking to be forgiven. Each had been prayed over, forgiven and sent home. They said that this pastoral response had been the least helpful to them because it had enabled them to continue to avoid accountability for their offences.[11] As we shall see later, not only was this bad and damaging practice on the part of their pastors but it was also based on a misunderstanding and confusion about the crucial distinction between forgiveness being offered and forgiveness being received. However, it is also relevant to reflect upon at this point because it refers to the timing of forgiveness.

We have considered some of the obstacles to the journey of offering forgiveness, but what helps the path? Certainly, seeing it *as* a path is crucial. Wanting to want to forgive marks its start. It matters that we know that we do not have to climb a mountain all in one day or at one go. It matters also that we know that we might never reach the top of the mountain. What is crucial is that we are on the journey, on the way, making what progress we can in our ascent at a speed that we can sustain, and a variable speed at that. It is being on the way that counts, not how far we have yet progressed or how fast.

It matters too that we understand that any forgiveness that we are able to show is towards the offenders, not their actions. Murder is murder and will always be wrong, as will terrorism, abuse, incest, slavery, or any of the extremes which we have been considering, but the lesser actions such as lying, stealing, wilfully omitting to do good, are all wrong. Forgiving is relational, shown to the person who has wronged us, not to their action or lack of it. Some people are not able to take any step towards forgiving because they think that, by forgiving, they are in some way being asked to say that the evil was not evil or the wrong not a wrong. Not so.

Seeing the one who has offended us as a person rather than a label or an object can help us to begin the path of offering forgiveness. While they remain the terrorist, the murderer, the slanderer, the bigot, the thief, then it is all the harder to see them as a human being, someone rather than something. Indeed, people will hold on to regarding the one who has wronged them as an object because they cannot begin to think that another human being could possibly have acted the way they did. This can all be part of coming to terms with and facing up to the pain. In the blame culture that we have seen growing in our social media especially, demonizing the other is more common than ever and makes seeing the other as the person they are even more difficult as a result.

It is nevertheless *people* who wrong us, *people* who hurt us, *people* who offend us. This is easier for us to see when we are wronged in a relatively slight way: a thoughtless jibe, missing an appointment, shouting or losing one's temper, not bothering to ask after someone or care for them properly when they are obviously upset, taking us for granted, criticizing unfairly or unkindly. These are all things we can easily do ourselves to other people. When we are on the receiving end of these things and know that we need to forgive the other person, then it is clear to us that we are needing to forgive someone who is just like ourselves. They may, of course, be a close friend or family member, someone we know very well and like or love, perhaps someone who has already, instantly, apologized for upsetting us. In these circumstances, seeing the one who has offended us as a person is not in itself difficult, which makes reaching out to them with forgiveness that much easier, though may be still less than straightforward, especially if the offence has been deliberately cutting or part of a repeated pattern.

If we are reluctant to see the one who causes us lesser griefs as a person and reach out to them in forgiveness, then we are even less likely to be able or want to do so towards the one who causes the bigger offences and hurts.

When we have ourselves been hurt it can sometimes help us to see the one who has hurt us as themselves a 'hurting person'.

We are all of us hurt and damaged in some regard; none of us is perfect, however good our parents or upbringing. The only way we can think or act is as the people we are, not the ones we might wish to be or present as being. That means that we think and act with and through our flaws and hurts and inevitably, to some degree, are prone to passing them on. Hurts beget hurts. Flaws cause more flaws. But love and forgiveness can overcome and are stronger.

It is all too familiar to us to look at situations of prejudice and discrimination, unemployment and poverty, broken homes and broken relationships, failing education and schools, as settings that can make violence or gangs or crime more likely. If we continue to create or allow such environments of hurt with hurting people in them, whether in our own country or others, then we continue as a society to have some shared responsibility for the hurts that are caused as a result. We all have grown and developed in response to the love and hate which we have experienced in the different situations and areas of our lives. There is a sense in which we are both loved and hated into being, as we respond to the positive or negative relationships and experiences that have touched us through infancy, childhood and adulthood. The positive ones build us up and let us flourish; the negative seek to diminish and belittle. Those who offend us are hurting people because we are all, to some extent, hurting people and contribute in some degree to the hurts of others and pass the hurts on.

If we can see something of this at work in our own lives, the lives of others and the world around us, then we are more able to see those who offend us as also offended against, people, human beings, in need of forgiveness, as we are. This is not in any way to equate directly one hurt with another, nor to say that the responsibility for our hurting others lies only with those who have contributed to our hurts: far from it. It is to say that the contributors to any single act of wrong are more diverse and varied than may appear at first sight to be the case, and that each shares some small, even miniscule, part, which is not to deny the responsibility or free will of the perpetrator or offender who ends up doing the hurt to us. It is the drops that make up the ocean, the individuals that make up the crowd, the single votes that create an election, the cells which make up our bodies:

always the many contributing to the single but damaged whole, though the contributions are by no means all of equal size or significance.

In Victor Hugo's *Les Misérables,* Bishop Myriel is robbed by the young Jean Valjean to whom he has given hospitality. When the police catch Jean Valjean and discover the bishop's silver in his bag, they take him back to the bishop who, to their amazement, tells them that he gave the silver to the young man. More than that, he asks Jean Valjean why he did not take the candlesticks as well and promptly gives him those, too. This classic expression of overwhelmingly generous forgiveness and love is the beginning of the transformation of Jean Valjean's life. It expresses the recklessness of unconditional love poured out to one who has been so damaged already in his young life. Bishop Myriel saw the thief as a human being in need of love and forgiveness and responded with an act which had untold repercussions, not just in the story of the novel itself but for all who have read it or seen a musical or stage version.

Bishop Myriel did not know enough of Jean Valjean's story to know quite why he stole, but he did know enough of human nature and his own times to understand that people may well steal out of a desperation forced upon them by injustices done to them by others. As we have seen above, Terry Waite wrote: 'If you can understand why people behave as they behave, at least you can be on the road to forgiveness.' We can only understand as we begin to see them as people, and then also to see something of their hurt. When Terry Waite returned to Beirut some years after his kidnapping and met his kidnappers, he referred to them as having been at the 'bottom of the pile'. He understood something of their situation, their motivation, their hurt. This did not excuse anything that had happened, but the understanding itself helped Terry Waite in the process of forgiving them.

We can be aided in seeing those who have offended us as people rather than labels, and then relating more to them as a result, if we can also grow in awareness of what has shaped us and in some of the gifts and advantages that we have received. Tradition has it that it was the sixteenth-century priest John Bradford who gave us the saying, 'There but for the grace of God, go I.' At the time, he was locked up in the Tower of London and saw a fellow prisoner being led to execution. Being able to empathize with others is more possible as we grow in self-awareness and insight.

That is not to say that we might ever be able to empathize with those who have hurt us terribly, though some achieve this. If the perpetrator was totally unknown to us, then empathy is unlikely ever to be possible unless, following on from what has happened, we take some steps to find out about them or even to meet. When the perpetrator was known to them, then some people record that it helped them to forgive by trying to remember back to a time before the offence, when they could recall some element of the relationship that was positive or kind. Seen through the lens of what happened subsequently, however, the motive for such behaviour might well become suspect.

Another aspect of the forgiving process that can assist the offering of forgiveness is knowing that the person who has offended us has shown remorse and apologized, though for more extreme offences this may well make little or no difference to a victim for some time because the pain, hurt and anger are still too great. Nevertheless, for the small offences done to us, if a person immediately says 'Sorry', and seems to mean it, then we are much more likely to say, 'That's OK', or similar. The same processes are at work as we offer forgiveness for little wrongs as for greater ones, though the scale, of course, makes a huge difference and the way and length of time that it takes for us to come to terms with what has happened may be of a different order.

There are many inspiring examples of people who have walked the path of offering forgiveness to those who have deeply offended them with terrible actions and hurts and have gone on to be able to meet the perpetrator and even have some sense of reconciliation. As we shall see in a later chapter, reconciliation is where the ends of the two journeys of offering and receiving forgiveness meet. It is likely always to be rare for such a point to be achievable, if only because it needs two to want the same goal and to walk to it.

Terry Waite and Lesley Bilinda both walked the path of offering forgiveness to those who had deeply and profoundly hurt them, and returned to where the offences had taken place, meeting the perpetrators. In Terry Waite's case, his journey took him back to Beirut, and in Lesley Bilinda's to Rwanda.

Jill Saward is another who had the courage to meet a person who had profoundly and terribly offended against her. When she was 21 and at home in Ealing, where her father was the vicar, a gang broke into the house, intent on robbery. Two of them raped her. She famously became the first rape victim to choose to forego her anonymity and spent the rest of her life campaigning on behalf of rape victims in the light of her own horrific experiences. The judge at the trial of the gang sparked outrage by saying that Jill Saward's trauma 'had not been so great' and sentenced the gang members who had raped her to fewer years than the one on trial who had not, appearing to value property more than Jill. By all accounts, the judge regretted his comment and judgement for the rest of his life.

When the convicted gang member who had not raped Jill came out of prison after ten years, he wanted to meet her. He said to her, 'I know I've got no right to ask your forgiveness.' She held his hand and replied, 'But you have it anyway. You've had it for a very long time.' She had earlier said: 'They'd destroyed enough. I didn't want them to destroy anything else. Forgiveness gave me that liberation, that freedom to move on.'

Jill Saward, who wrote a book about her experiences, *Rape: My Story*, continued to refer to the balaclaved men who had attacked her and been sent to prison as Man 1, Man 2 and Man 3, even though she knew their names, because she did not wish to give them status by naming them.

When Jill Saward was interviewed by Elizabeth Grice of the *Daily Telegraph* 30 years after the attack, she said, 'It's not a question of whether you can or can't forgive. It's a question of whether you will or won't.' David Kerr, who was Jill's boyfriend at the time of the attack and who was himself beaten up, said of her, 'She was able to forgive and turn something horrific into a positive.'[12]

Another person who met someone who had done violence to her earlier in her life was Cornelia (Corrie) ten Boom, the daughter of a Dutch watchmaker who, together with her sister Betsie and their family, had offered shelter to persecuted Jews and others needing sanctuary during the Second World War, following the German invasion of the Netherlands. There was constant danger and threat of discovery for the ten Booms who risked everything for the sake of helping those in need. Their work became known to the Dutch Resistance who sent an architect to their house in order to construct a secret room, next to Corrie ten Boom's own room, for the Jews to use as a hiding place. There was also an alert buzzer installed in the house to warn the refugees to get into the room as quickly as possible in cases of danger.

The family and its work were eventually informed against, leading to the arrest of them all, though the six Jews and resistance workers that they were housing at the time got into the secret hiding place and were not found or arrested but transferred to safety a few days later by the Resistance. Corrie's and Betsie's father, Casper, died ten days after their arrest. Having been initially in Scheveningen prison, they were moved to Herzogenbusch, Kamp Vught, and later to Ravensbruck. They were sustained in the camps, as they had been in their work of giving sanctuary to the Jews and others, by their profound Christian faith. Shortly after arriving at Vught, Betsie said to Corrie:

'"If people can be taught to hate, they can be taught to love! We must find the way, you and I, no matter how long it takes." She went on, almost forgetting in her excitement to keep her voice to a whisper, while I slowly took in the fact that she was talking about our guards. I glanced at the matron seated at the desk ahead of us. I saw a gray uniform and a visored hat: Betsie saw a wounded human being.'[13]

Even while they were in Ravensbruck, the two sisters were discussing plans for creating a place of healing after the war. Betsie had a vision of what the house that they would use would be like. Later, she also had a vision of a former concentration camp in Germany to be used as well. Both visions were later fulfilled as both properties were used.

Betsie died in Ravensbruck but Corrie was released just over a fortnight after, due to what was discovered later to have been a clerical error. After the war she continued her work, turning a beautiful mansion in Bloemendaal, given by Mrs Bierens de Haan, into a rehabilitation centre and home. 'For all these people alike,' wrote Corrie ten Boom, 'the key to healing turned out to be the same. Each had a hurt he had to forgive: the neighbour who had reported him, the brutal guard, the sadistic soldier.'[14]

Corrie ten Boom found herself being invited to travel all over the world to speak about her experiences, her work and her faith. On one occasion, she was speaking at a church service in Munich when she saw someone she recognized as having been an SS guard in Ravensbruck. She wrote:

He was the first of our actual jailers that I had seen since that time. And suddenly it was all there – the roomful of mocking men, the heaps of clothing, Betsie's pain-blanched face.

He came up to me as the church was emptying, beaming and bowing. 'How grateful I am for your message Fraulein,' he said. 'To think that, as you say, He has washed my sins away!'

His hand was thrust out to shake mine. And I, who had preached so often to the people in Bloemendaal the need to forgive, kept my hand at my side.

Even as the angry, vengeful thoughts boiled through me, I saw the sin of them. Jesus Christ died for this man; was I going to ask for more? Lord Jesus, I prayed, forgive me and help me to forgive him.

I tried to smile, I struggled to raise my hand. I could not. I felt nothing, not the slightest spark of warmth or charity. And so again I breathed a silent prayer. Jesus, I cannot forgive him. Give me Your forgiveness.

As I took his hand the most incredible thing happened. From my shoulder along my arm and through my hand a current seemed to pass from me to him, while into my heart sprang a love for this stranger that almost overwhelmed me.

And so I discovered that it is not on our forgiveness any more than our goodness that the world's healing hinges, but on His. When He tells us to love our enemies, He gives, along with the command, the love itself.[15]

Corrie ten Boom's experience of meeting a former prison guard at a church service is matched by that of Bishop Leonard Wilson, the Anglican Bishop of Singapore from 1941. He was interned in the notorious Changi prison and later accused of being a spy and tortured.

Bishop Leonard's daughter, Canon Susan Cole-King, was invited to preach to all the archbishops and bishops of the Anglican

Communion gathered at the Lambeth Conference in 1998, where she said about her father:

He was accused of being a spy and for many days he was subjected to torture. Often, he had to be carried back to the crowded, dark and filthy cell, almost unconscious from his wounds. On one occasion, when seven men were taking it in turns to flog him, they asked him why he didn't curse them. He told them it was because he was a follower of Jesus who taught us to love one another. He asked himself then how he could possibly love these men with their hard, cruel faces, who were obviously enjoying the torture they were inflicting. As he prayed, he had a picture of them as they might have been as little children, and it's hard to hate little children. But then, more powerfully, his prayer was answered by some words of a well-known communion hymn which came to his mind: 'Look, Father, look on his anointed face, and only look on us as found in him.' In that moment he was given a vision of those men not as they were then, but as they were capable of becoming, transformed by the love of Christ. He said he saw them completely changed, their cruelty becoming kindness, their sadistic instincts changed to gentleness. Although he felt it was too blasphemous to use Christ's words 'Father, forgive them,' he experienced the grace of forgiveness at that moment. After eight months he was released back to Changi – one of the few who survived. For the rest of his life he emphasized in his speaking and preaching the importance of forgiveness.

Bishop Leonard survived his remaining time in Changi, returning to England at the end of the war where he exercised his ministry as a bishop in Birmingham Diocese. He did, however, return to Singapore and during that visit had the great joy of confirming one of his torturers. He described the moment:

One of these men who was allowed to march up from the prison to the cathedral, as a prisoner, to come for baptism, was one of those who had stood with a rope in his hand, threatening and sadistic. I have seldom seen so great a change in a man. He looked gentle and peaceful. His face was completely changed by the power of Christ.

Canon Cole-King went on in her address to thank the Japanese archbishop and bishops, who were there in front of her, for the apology that they had made earlier that day in the Conference,[16] and to say that true reconciliation 'can only happen when there is an acknowledgement of wrongs done, when the truth is faced, and painful self-examination leads to confession and apology'. She referred to the cycle of reconciliation being complete: her father with his torturer, she and her brothers with the Japanese bishops. She was preaching on 6 August, the feast of the Transfiguration of Christ and the anniversary of the dropping of the atomic bomb on Hiroshima. Because the day is about both disfiguring and transfiguring, Susan Cole-King ended her address with some words of the theologian Karl Barth:

> Thus, our tribulation without ceasing to be tribulation is transformed. We suffer as we suffered before, but our suffering is no longer a passive perplexity but is transformed into a pain which is creative, fruitful, full of power and promise. The road which is impassable has been made known to us in the crucified and risen Lord.

Transforming a pain into something creative, full of power and promise, is what forgiveness and reconciliation are all about. Like the others whom we have been considering, Eric Lomax discovered this truth as well. For him, as for the others, it was indeed a costly and painful path. We have already referred to his recurrent nightmares for more than 50 years following his terrible torture as a prisoner of war. He had been captured in Siam (Thailand) with thousands of other British soldiers in February 1942 and made to work on the building of the Burma railway but after a radio had been discovered by the Japanese in the camp where he was in Kanburi, he and others were tortured to try to get them to reveal details of the radio. Eric Lomax was beaten and waterboarded, had ribs and limbs broken, was shut into a minute cell, which became like an oven in the sun and was too small for him even to lie across diagonally. He was denied food and water and brutally treated, yet somehow he survived. Throughout the months of torture and imprisonment in Outram Road he had had the same Japanese interpreter acting for the Kempeitai, the Japanese secret police.

Despite all that happened to him, Eric Lomax came through the war and eventually returned to England where he spent two more years in the army before working in the Colonial Office and then retraining in personnel management. He retired in 1982 but had already decided that he needed to try to search out the truth of what had happened in Kanburi. With the encouragement of his wife Patti, he wrote an article in the London 'FEPOW Forum', which was read by fellow FEPOWs (Far Eastern Prisoners of War), appealing for information about what had happened over 40 years earlier. By this means, Eric found himself in touch again with Jim Bradley whom he had known in Changi. He went to stay with him in 1989 and Jim's wife Lindy gave him a photocopy of an article from the *Japan Times* of 15 August 1989, an English-language paper, published in Tokyo, which she had been sent by the War Graves Commission in Japan.

The article was about Mr Nagase Takashi who, after the war, had helped the Allied armies in their search for the graves of those who died in Thailand along the railway. The article, which included a photograph of Nagase, quoted him as saying that he had flashbacks of Japanese military police in Kanchanaburi torturing a POW who was accused of possessing a map of the railway. Eric Lomax realized that he had found the interrogator who had contributed so much to his torture. He wrote:

I had apparently found one of the men I was looking for and I had the near certainty ... that I knew who he was and where he was. I was in such a strong position: I could if I wished reach out and touch him, to do him real harm.

Lomax went on: 'I wanted to see Nagase's sorrow so that I could live better with my own ... I was not inclined to forgive, not yet, and probably never.'[17] This was the man of whom he had written:

I wanted to do violence to them, thinking quite specifically of how I would like to revenge myself on the goon squad from Kanburi and the hateful little interrogator from the Kempeitai with his dreadful English pronunciation, his mechanical questions and his way of being in the room yet seeming to be detached from it. I wished to drown him, cage him and beat him, to see how he liked it. I still thought of his voice, his slurred elocution: 'Lomax, you will be killed shortly'; 'Lomax, you will tell us'; you remember phrases from encounters that have hurt you, and my meetings with him were cast in a harsh light.[18]

Over the next few years, Eric Lomax tried to decide what to do with the information that he now had and the power that he felt that it gave him over his adversary. He was 'consumed by the desire to make Nagase suffer fully the consequences of his actions',[19] and planned to use the opportunity of a film that was going to be made to arrange a meeting with Nagase, but without disclosing beforehand exactly who he was.

Over the following months, Eric Lomax found several things worked to change his attitude completely, much to his own amazement. First, he met a Japanese researcher, the first Japanese person he had known for over 45 years. She was interested in his memories and he became fascinated by her as a first new contact with Japan and his own past. This was followed by his being given a copy of a book, *Crosses and Tigers*, written by Nagase himself and translated into English. Lomax said that he read the book with a 'surprising sense of detachment', despite it describing his own torture, but when Patti read it she was filled with anger and wanted immediately to draft a letter to Nagase. The letter she sent had as a final paragraph:

My husband has lived all these years with the after effects of the cruel experiences he suffered and I hope that contact between you could be a healing experience for both of you. How can you feel 'forgiven' Mr. Nagase, if this particular former Far Eastern prisoner-of-war has not yet forgiven you? My husband does understand the cultural pressures you were under during the war but whether he can totally forgive your own involvement remains to be seen and it is not for me, who was not there, to judge ...[20]

When Eric Lomax read Nagase Takashi's letter replying to Patti's, he wrote:

Patti thought this was an extraordinarily beautiful letter. Anger drained away; in its place came a welling of compassion for both Nagase and for me, coupled with a deep sense of sadness and regret. In that moment I lost whatever hard armour I had wrapped around me and began to think the unthinkable: that I could meet Nagase face to face in simple good will. Forgiveness became more than an abstract idea: it was now a real possibility.[21]

Eric Lomax had begun to see the Japanese as people and his own torturer as a person, a fellow human being with feelings and deep remorse, one who had in his own way also suffered. The more he saw him like this and the more that Patti and he corresponded with Nagase Takashi, the less he wanted to kill or even hurt him. They decided that they wanted to meet in Thailand and then go on to Japan together. As soon as they could, they arranged to meet on the River Kwae Bridge by Kanchanaburi, right next to where Nagase had opened a Buddhist temple of peace as part of his own charitable work of atoning. Even up to the last minute, Eric Lomax wanted to hold on to that power, and in that sense, too, the 'advantage', as he saw it, of being there first so that he could see Nagase approach before Nagase saw him. Nagase bowed low in the formal Japanese manner and, trembling, with tears in his eyes, said over and over again, 'I am very, very sorry.'

Eric Lomax was determined now not only to forgive Nagase but to do so in a fitting, formal way, so when they were in Japan he read him a short letter that he had written, which ended up assuring him of his 'total forgiveness'.

After this, Eric Lomax, the former prisoner of war who had been so terribly beaten, starved and tortured, wrote of his former tormentor and persecutor as his 'friend' and that meeting him had turned him from a hated enemy into a 'blood-brother'.

Few people who have suffered terribly are ever able to meet

their tormentor and forgive them, and even fewer be reconciled so that they can become friends, but the experience of Eric Lomax and Nagase Takashi shows that it is possible. Perhaps they needed the 50 years after the torture and war for their reconciliation to be achievable. They certainly needed to meet and see the other as a vulnerable, damaged person who had borne and was still bearing great suffering. They also needed to want resolution, peace, forgiveness and reconciliation. In Nagase Takashi's case that had become strongly linked to his Buddhist faith; in Eric Lomax's it went back to his own Christian roots and faith.

So why do people forgive? What are the motivations? Certainly, faith can be and frequently is a strong driver. It was there for Terry Waite, Lesley Bilinda, Gordon Wilson, Jill Saward, Corrie ten Boom, Bishop Leonard Wilson, Susan Cole-King, Nagase Takashi and Eric Lomax, as for so very many others. There has to be the recognition that revenge is no answer, that ultimately it never 'works'. The Old Testament teaching of an 'eye for eye',[22] which was intended to be setting the limit to retaliation of *only* an eye and not more, risks even so turning the whole world blind. Revenge cannot make up for hurts done, pain experienced, life lost, sufferings endured, tragic consequences borne, disfigurement and illness. There must be another and better way, and of course there is.

But how are we to find it? What is to motivate us to take it? Do we have to be at rock bottom before we are motivated to find a route back?

For some it may be necessary to reach the extremes and plumb the depths of despair or pain or exhaustion before an alternative way is found; thankfully for most that does not have to be the path. The signs can be read much earlier; the memories of previous, even if lesser, issues can chart our steps; the examples of others whom we know or about whom we have heard can be an inspiration; someone who hurt us but then reaches out to us with deep remorse and sincere apology; our philosophy of life, and of course our faith, can be our guide. The reason for our risking the way of forgiveness may be a combination of different factors and frequently is, including perhaps our own self-interest as we increasingly come to see the alternative as being a dead end, leading us nowhere other than to yet more prolonged pain and 'imprisonment'. As Eric Lomax had put it, 'The privacy of the torture victim is more impregnable than any island fortress.'[23]

A deeply moving account of how someone is motivated to offer forgiveness by her faith, but also by the realization that all is not well in her relationships, is given by Kristin Jacks, Country Director of Servants to Asia's Urban Poor, Cambodia.

Chrang Bak is a village built on the rubbish-strewn edge of the Bassac river near Phnom Penh, in Cambodia. Om Kheun is a local shopkeeper. Perhaps she is a better neighbour than businesswoman, because when poor neighbours come to buy food on credit, she cannot refuse. People from all over the neighbourhood come to her for advice as well as goods. She understands their problems because she is poor too.

Om Kheun later became a Christian. She read in the Bible that Jesus calls us to forgive those who have wronged us. With this new insight, she examined her heart and saw that there was something wrong there, something that was spoiling her relationships in the village. Over the years she had extended a lot of credit to other families. The amounts had grown so large that few of the poorest families would ever be able to repay her. And this created a double problem. Deep down she realized she felt angry and frustrated with those who owed her so much. She could be so much further ahead in life if they paid up! On the other hand, she realized that those poor families were also deeply ashamed of their debt and they now avoided her as much as possible. Om Kheun didn't want to feel bitter, or to be avoided. And so, inspired by what she read in the Bible, she decided to solve the problem. Taking her record book in hand, she went from family to family and before their eyes drew a line through their debt, declaring it 'forgiven'. At the stroke of a pen they were set free – and so now was she.

Although her life is often a struggle, Om Kheun has a sense of freedom. She has found something better than bitterness and hatred. She found a faith that transformed her despair into hope through the power of love and forgiveness.'[24]

Om Kheun 'examined her heart'. She became aware of many issues, which all had a bearing on her life and debt, relationships and well-being. Furthermore, what began from her sense of being wronged by others enabled her to see that she herself harboured some anger and frustration towards them which was mutually damaging. Om Kheun 'didn't want to feel bitter', and she knew the way out and took it.

Om Kheun was very clear to those whose debt she forgave. She did not just cross out the debt or just tell them she was going to do so, but went to each in turn and did it in front of them, for them to see and witness. This prompts the question as to whether forgiveness must be offered explicitly or not. How far can implicit forgiveness be relied upon?

In his novel *Love Story*, Eric Segal has two of his characters say, 'Love means never having to say you're sorry.'[25] Does this mean that where there is love, there is always forgiveness and so there is no need to apologize? Or maybe it means that where there is love there will never be any hurts that need either apology or forgiving, though that seems even less likely. Either way, it is surely wrong. It should be the case that love will always forgive, but that does not mean that no apology is needed. It is important that we acknowledge our wrongdoing and take responsibility for it, otherwise we tend to justify ourselves and put ourselves in the right over against others, even those whom we love.

We were recognizing earlier that there can be a restoration of international relationships between countries that have been at war without formal apologies or statements of forgiveness, but this transfers less easily to individual relationships where a more explicit expression is likely to be needed. However, where there is a closeness of relationship between two people and where apology and forgiveness are familiar, then something more implicit becomes possible. Also, other actions can speak very loudly and clearly at times, expressing the offer of forgiveness, without the need for words.

In the Gospel of St John, we are given the account of Jesus appearing to the disciple Peter after the resurrection and, therefore, after Peter's threefold denial of even knowing him, let alone following him and being a friend. The very fact that the risen Christ appears at all to his disciples is an expression of forgiveness and continuing, faithful love for those who deserted and denied him. In Peter's case, the conversation that Jesus initiates carries an even clearer expression of forgiveness as Jesus asks three times if Peter loves him. He who said 'No' those three times is now given the opportunity to say 'Yes' three times. Jesus then goes further in expressing complete restoration and forgiveness by commissioning him for the key role among the disciples.

Peter, who had wept after his denials of Jesus, knew that he was not only still loved but completely forgiven and healed, made stronger than before by the experience. For most of us in most situations when we have wronged another person, there is a need for us to know unequivocally that we are forgiven, just as there is a need for us, when we have been wronged, to express clearly our forgiveness. If the person who has wronged us is dead at the time we reach a point of being able and wanting to articulate our forgiveness of them, then all we can do is know in our own hearts the offer of forgiveness, and perhaps let others know of this as well as taking it to God in our prayers.

Before we complete this look at the journey of offering forgiveness we need to acknowledge that, tragically, it is possible to use the offer of forgiveness itself in a distorted way. A small number of those who have been traumatized as victims see the offering of forgiveness as an opportunity to exert some control over their offender, perhaps even revenge. They take pleasure in attaching conditions to the forgiveness and in seeking to put themselves in a position of strength with the threat of withdrawing the offer if their stated conditions are not met. Even Eric Lomax, with the extraordinary level of forgiveness and reconciliation which he achieved with his torturer, wanted to keep some power and advantage over his adversary along the way to that place of mutual healing.

If offering forgiveness can on rare occasions be manipulative, so too can false expressions of remorse and apology be used manipulatively as a devious attempt to continue contact with and control over victims. Those who have been convicted of extreme crimes are usually, for this reason, banned from making any contact with their victims. Understandable and perhaps necessary though this may be, it also has, as a consequence, the stopping of heartfelt and genuine apology and remorse which might have made the process of offering forgiveness slightly easier were it to have been known. In one extraordinary case, it might even have saved a life.

Kayla Greenwood wrote to the Governor of Arkansas on 27 April 2017 asking him to spare the life of the man who had killed her father. Kenneth Williams was due to be executed that same night, but the family of his victim had not known. Nor had they known that he had appealed for clemency and that they could have testified at his clemency hearing on his behalf if they had been aware.

In her letter, Kayla Greenwood told the Governor that she had learnt that Kenneth Williams had a daughter, Jasmine, who was a similar age to herself. It transpired that Jasmine had been appealing for funds to enable her and her own daughter to afford to travel to see her father one last time before he was executed. Kayla's family not only paid for the flight to enable the meeting to take place but Kayla herself picked them up at the airport and drove them to the prison, waiting while they went in. She wrote to Governor Hutchinson:

> Watching her leave the prison and knowing that was probably their last goodbye broke my heart. Jasmine had done nothing at all but like me, she could lose her father. If Mr. Williams is executed, her loss, her pain will be as real as mine. I do not wish this on anyone.
>
> Jasmine told me that when she saw her father and talked to him she knew he was a different man. He was a man of love and gratitude for the opportunity to say his last goodbye. I have come to learn that he is a man who counsels and helps people who may be in a dark place because they never felt love, or were victims of a horrible upbringing that caused trauma and hurt.
>
> Because he once knew that same dark place, Mr. Williams could connect and show people that from even the darkest of places, you can always come out and change and help others to see right from wrong.
>
> Being there for others, no matter what, and showing what true pure unconditional love is and feels like, that is the closest we can get to God in this physical world. I know Mr. Williams has and will change people he meets for the better and alive, he can make a positive difference and I believe that is the most beautiful story of justice.

I also believe in second, even third chances because I know people can change.

You often hear stories of men who go into prison and become bitter, angry and hateful. I do not believe Mr. Williams is one of those men. He found God and I believe his redemption is genuine. Mr. Williams is not the person who killed my father on October 4, 1999. It is the changed man, the new Kenneth Williams that we are asking you to save.

My family also requested an opportunity to meet with Mr. Williams but it was denied. We just wanted to tell him that we forgave him and thought it was important to do that face to face. It would be one way to get closure.[26]

Tragically, despite this letter, Kenneth Williams was given a lethal injection and died late on 27 April 2017, though he was made aware of the Greenwood family's forgiveness and, of course, their generosity in paying for his daughter and granddaughter to be able to see him before he died. He described this as a 'blast of glorious light' which no one could withstand and 'continue to walk in darkness'.[27]

5

Receiving forgiveness

A further barrier to the offering of forgiveness for some is that they think that if they do forgive the one who has wronged them criminally, then that person will 'get off scot-free'. This, however, is to misunderstand the nature of forgiveness by conflating the offering of forgiveness with the receiving of forgiveness and assuming that the one automatically happens with the other. Nevertheless, there are many who still think that offering forgiveness gives rise to an injustice for precisely that reason. However, if forgiveness is to be received fully in such circumstances, then that can only happen with justice being done, because of the nature of the journey and process of receiving forgiveness. As with the offering of forgiveness, so with the receiving: both are journeys, both have very different stages and elements along the way. What they also have in common is that we may not reach the end of either journey in our lifetime. What matters most is that we are on the way and travelling.

It is worth registering again that seeking to set down in words what are the different elements involved in the journey of forgiveness carries the danger of making the whole process appear far too ordered, too clinical, too neat and tidy. We all know that it is not like that at all and that there is an inherent messiness and lack of ordered path or sequence. Ultimately, there will be many elements coming together if forgiveness is to be fully received, just as there are many elements coming together for forgiveness to be fully offered, but the way they do that and when they do that will be unique for each person.

With that warning and caveat constantly in mind, it is possible to identify seven elements that need to be in place for the journey of receiving forgiveness to be travelled its full length to the final stage, reconciliation, though the sequencing of the elements will vary greatly from person to person, case to case, as will the speed of travel.

Recognition

If ever forgiveness is to be received, then that can only happen for something which we recognize and acknowledge that we have done. If we are blamed for something which is not our responsibility, there is clearly nothing for which we need to be forgiven, even though we or another person may think initially that there is. However, if we have done something, or at least contributed to it, but fail or refuse to recognize the fact, then we cannot begin to receive forgiveness, even though we need it. There must be no place for obfuscation, denial, ignoring, dismissing, compartmentalizing, burying, excusing, pretending, justifying or sustaining illusions. We have to admit, or at least begin to admit, that something wrong has taken place and that 'I am involved'.

This step is akin to judgement: it involves a person discerning and accepting that actions for which they were responsible have caused pain, hurt, perhaps even trauma, to one or more other people. It is crucial not to play down the seriousness of what has transpired, just as it is important not to exaggerate it either or take wrong responsibility for it. Recognition needs honesty and a balanced, fair judgement, neither overstating nor underplaying the significance of what has happened and certainly not excusing or minimalizing it. Only when the facts are looked at can we see that something wrong has taken place. This, of course, may well not happen at the time of the wrong itself but subsequently. In some cases, this will be because, at the moment of causing the offence, we were totally absorbed in ourselves or completely oblivious to others or convinced that we were right, and so not open to looking at all objectively and seeing the truth. In other situations, it may only be with hindsight that we realize that we could have done something to help, or should have done but failed to do so. Also, it is possible that, at the time that we caused injury to someone else, we were acting in good faith on the facts as we knew and understood them to be, but only later came to see that we had been wrongly informed. If this was through no fault of our own, then, in such circumstances, although we were involved in the causing of the injury, the responsibility will not have been with us and there will not be anything for which we need forgiving. Very often, recognition of the truth of what has happened only comes about through the intervention of someone else or through our reflecting subsequently or listening to our conscience.

There is a telling story in the Old Testament about King David who has arranged for the husband of a woman with whom he commits adultery to be killed in battle. He then finds that he has a visitor, the prophet Nathan, who tells him a story of a rich man with many flocks and herds taking the only lamb of a poor man to feed a visitor. David is outraged and says that the man who has behaved like that deserves to die. 'You are the man!', says Nathan to him. Only then can David recognize and admit that he has done so very wrong in having Uriah the Hittite killed.[1]

Jesus' parables and stories are in the same tradition as the prophet Nathan. They encourage us to recognize, honestly, more about ourselves. What kind of soil are you in the parable of the sower?[2] Are you more like the prodigal, younger son or his older brother?[3] More like the priest, the Levite or the Samaritan?[4] Are you a sheep or a goat?[5]

Sometimes we need another person to hold up a mirror for us to see ourselves a little bit more as we really are. Sometimes it comes about through our being challenged more directly. Sometimes it simply needs us to have space to reflect and think and imagine in order to know ourselves more as we really are and less as we pretend or want ourselves to be.

Our conscience can play a vital role in this and is helped by our practising the art of listening to it rather than ignoring it or even trying to kill it, if such a thing is possible. Space and silence, prayer, meditation and mindfulness can all help to enable us to hear our conscience better and more loudly.

Self-examination is not often encouraged as once it was but can still play a helpful and important part in our self-awareness and recognition of what we have done wrong or failed to do. Prayer manuals used to suggest that people spent time reflecting silently about all the different areas and relationships of their life and trying to see each part in turn through the lens of the Ten

Commandments (Ex. 20.1–17), or the Lord's Prayer (Matt. 6.9–13) or the Beatitudes (Matt. 5.1–12) or the seven deadly sins. Looking in this way can help us to be realistic and honest in our view of ourselves, but it needs us to make time to do so.

Consciences can be either sharpened or blunted depending upon how much we listen to them and how well or badly we treat them. If they are continually squashed and ignored they become blunter, just as attending to what they are saying to us helps sharpen their insight. Our reflection on what is right and wrong helps shape and inform our consciences, which are not static and immutable, but capable of change and development as our own views alter, as well as those of the social context in which we find ourselves living. We need, therefore, to make an active choice as to how we want our conscience to evolve, rather than just let it drift as the societal winds of change blow over us. This is partly why teachers of prayer will recommend that we examine ourselves and our consciences. In the process, we are strengthened in the choosing of what is right and true and in the opposing of what is wrong.

Our self-examination also helps us see how our behaviour affects others. Our actions have a bearing on others, even if it is only by changing us and how we relate. If there is something of which we are ashamed, then it will make us less open with others and ourselves. If there is something we are hiding, then it will make us more secretive, more guarded and less forthcoming with others.

Our recognition of what we are really like, and what we have done and failed to do, lets us see ourselves and our actions in the light rather than hide them in the dark. One of our children, when they were very small, announced at a meal that they were going under the table to pick their nose. It is basic within us that we hide to do the things which we know we should not be doing, whether they are little issues or big ones. We sense that they are 'of the dark' rather than 'of the light'. Adam and Eve hid in the Garden of Eden after they had eaten of the forbidden fruit.[6] No one taught them to hide or told them to do so. They just did it. We cannot recognize one another, let alone our actions, in the dark. We need the light. This is why the theme of light is so powerful and strong in the Gospels and in our understanding of judgement.[7] If we are to recognize our faults, failings, omissions and wrongs, then we need them to be out of the dark and in the light so as to see them properly.

Responsibility

Once we see ourselves more clearly in the light, then we are able as well to distinguish which parts of what has happened are our responsibility and which parts are not. Our blame culture wants to suggest that everything is our fault, or nothing is, but that of course is far from the reality. Even in the extreme cases of child abuse, there is far greater recognition than there was of cycles of abuse and with it the understanding that, however unlikely it may seem at first, very often abusers have themselves been abused.[8] Even if that is the tragic case, it does not stop the abuser from having some major responsibility for what they have done, but it does point to the fact that it is not totally their fault and there are long tentacles reaching in every direction as others share something of that terrible responsibility.

We know, similarly, that those brought up in homes with an alcoholic parent are more likely to drink to excess themselves. If they do, that does not mean that they have no responsibility for their own drinking, but it does mean that not all the responsibility is theirs. It is the same with gambling or over-eating. The responsibility for anything we do is rarely, if ever, 100 per cent ours. This is not to evade responsibility or pretend that something is not our fault but rather to seek to be honest about where the moral responsibility lies and acknowledge how complicated are the paths and relationships that shape our development.

In the 1980s, the Church of England was debating whether it was right to permit people who had been divorced and wanted to marry again to be able to have a further marriage in church. The Divorce Reform Act of 1969 had brought to an end the legal use of the language of 'guilty' and 'innocent' parties and only recognized the irretrievable breakdown of a marriage as the reason for divorce to be granted. I can recall a Methodist minister saying to me at the time, deliberately provocatively, that they would not marry the 'innocent' party on the basis that, if a husband or wife believed themselves to be innocent and their spouse totally guilty, then they should not get married again because they clearly had not learnt from their first marriage and so were very likely to end up divorced once more. Both parties contribute in some way to the breakdown of marriage or indeed any relationship, even if the overwhelming responsibility lies with one rather than the other. If we think that it is possible to be completely innocent and the fault to lie completely with the other person, then we have not understood the way that relationships work or our own part in them, and, as my Methodist minister friend implied, we are likely to repeat our mistakes. Seeing at least something of the complexity and, therefore, something of the responsibilities, is vital if we are to develop and grow strong and healthy relationships.

Just as we can trace some of the most strongly formative influences, people, experiences and relationships which have nurtured and shaped us in our lives, so, also, we can identify, increasingly, the gene sequences of our inherited characteristics. This makes it tempting for some to cross from an ethical language of responsibility as accounting for our actions to a biochemical language of genetics, shaping why we are the way we are. Biochemical, psychological, relational, historical and social descriptions can all be given of something that has happened and will play their part in aiding our understanding of the complete picture, but none of them removes or weakens the appropriateness of the moral description helping us to understand where responsibility lies. None of the other accounts can be used as an excuse for why we did what we did, even if they do help illuminate some of the varied influences upon us. Responsibility must be recognized and admitted, or at least our rightful share of the responsibility, for that alone is the part for which we can and need to be forgiven.

There is a telling phrase in the Ten Commandments which refers to 'the third and the fourth generation'[9] suffering the consequences of the parents' actions, which is surely an indication of the complexity of the lines and threads of responsibility passed down from parent to child, to grandchild to great-grandchild. In such a web, there is no way in which we could identify all the complex strands and the part that each influence has played, even if we wished to do so. What we can do is recognize that responsibility is far more widely spread than we may be inclined to think and also that none of us is innocent, free from contributing in some degree to the wrongs that we ourselves and many others commit.

The recognition of the web in which each of us is caught up, simply by virtue of our birth and upbringing, relates as well to the observation we have already made about there being 'hurting people' who all too often pass on the hurt in some form or other, and also to the way in which each of us is 'loved and hated into being'.

Owning up to our responsibility is frequently neither easy nor comfortable. As with other parts of our journeying, if we have not learnt the way in childhood and adolescence, then learning to admit responsibilities for our adult faults will be all the harder. It is far from easy, too, to do so when the responsibility has been wrongly laid already at someone else's door and they are being blamed for what is our fault. Coming forward in such circumstances needs not only a high degree of honesty but also courage and readiness to accept the consequences.

Just as it requires honesty to admit to what are genuinely our failings, so also sometimes it needs honesty to realize that something for which we are blaming ourselves may not actually be our fault.

In the film *Good Will Hunting*, the psychologist Sean Maguire finally gets through to Will Hunting that all the things for which he is blaming himself are not his responsibility. He repeats over and over again, 'It's not your fault.' What Will partly knows with his head he begins to accept for the first time in his heart and, as a result, starts to cry. Will's head and heart begin at last to come together. For all of us, recognizing and admitting our responsibility must happen at every level of our being, not just our heads but our hearts and imaginations too.

Remorse

Will Hunting's tears were born out of emotional release as the truth sank down into him more fully and began to free him from the prison of his own self-blame and profound inner pain, enabling him to acknowledge what was deep within. Like water beginning to trickle past a frozen blockage as it thaws, enabling more to flow until the ice fully melts, so the first tears flowed and the dam was breached. In Will's case, the emotional pain was to do with what others had done to him, but it needed that connection of head and heart. When we come to understand with our hearts and imaginations, as well as our heads, something of the pain we have caused others by our actions, or at least to which we have contributed, then we can find ourselves crying for them and not just for ourselves. Such is the nature of remorse, of our lamenting what we have done. The more we feel the pain of those we have injured, the more we shall also commit to not repeating, and the more we are likely to learn and change.

Just as those who would learn to offer forgiveness must acknowledge the pain and hurt done to them, so those who would receive forgiveness must also acknowledge the pain and hurt which they have caused, or to which they have at least contributed, and experience something of the costliness of what they have done. Again, this involves our feelings and emotions as well as our thoughts.

In some cases, the pain of the one we have hurt is all too evident, as, for example, in a car crash or violent assault, but more commonly it will be hidden from view and taken into the privacy of the other person's life, which is why it needs our imagination to be at work to picture a little of what may be going on in their inner life and the damage that we have caused. In this, as in so much else, our conscience comes to our aid. It may prick us or, more strongly even, stab us, but only if we listen to it and let it convict us. In this, our conscience will be coupled healthily with our sense of guilt.

There are those who choose to give all guilt a bad press as though we should somehow learn to rise above it and outgrow it because it is a relic of the past, wanting to stop us doing what we want and restricting our freedom. It is certainly the case that there is false guilt from which we do need to be delivered because it ensnares, belonging to a cycle of blame and shame. It is associated very often with victimhood and feeling constrained to take the blame for every eventuality. Sometimes it will be motivated by a fear of not wanting to risk acknowledging or expressing genuine and legitimate anger, criticism or annoyance towards another person lest they are upset and punish us by withdrawing their affection. In these circumstances, it may well come about through a deep sense of neither being loved nor of feeling worthy to be loved. False guilt is associated with self-blame and self-hate, a lack of worth and a sense of shame. It frequently arises from our telling ourselves what we imagine we ought or should be doing in order to win longed-for praise and affirmation from others by whom it has been denied. As a result, unhealthy and false guilt is frequently coupled with an imagined but unattainable perfectionism where all, somehow, would be well.

Healthy guilt, by contrast, tells us when we have offended against another and are right to be pained by what we have done because our actions or thoughts were simply wrong or unkind, thoughtless, mean or selfish. The remedy is in repentance, in saying sorry and making amends in so far as it is open to us to do so.

This kind of guilt can be regarded as spiritual pain, calling out for us to stop hurting ourselves and others and to do something about it to put matters right again. It needs us to listen to it and act upon it rather than dismiss or avoid it. It links with the healthy pain of remorse and leads us onwards in our journey of receiving forgiveness.

Repentance

If we recognize something of the wrong we have done, accept our share of responsibility and feel remorse and regret for our actions, then we shall always want to go further and seek to make some amends. We shall see what has happened in a different way from the view we had at the time of the offence, perhaps now seeing it in the light rather than hiding in the dark. This is a change of perspective, a change of mind or heart. That is precisely what repentance means. At the time, we may have thought that what we were doing was right, or known it to be wrong but thought that we would get away with it, or more probably did not give it that amount of thought at all. Now we see it through different eyes, in a new way. We are not the person we were; we are changed. Where the fault or failing was small, the change may be small. Where the fault or failing was large, so may be the change brought about by repentance.

We are called to this change, this way of repentance. We are called to live it continually because we slip back and fail again, repeatedly. As Professor Gillian Rose put it, we are constantly 'failing towards' a continuous *metanoia* (repentance). Once more, it needs us to learn it, to practise it as a way of life.

Though our repentance needs voicing in most cases, with those whom we know well it may be that we develop a less explicit but helpfully understood code. Certainly, with those whom we have offended but know less well or not at all, our change of heart and remorse does need expressing. Quite how we apologize must depend upon what is helpful for the one or ones we have harmed, bearing in mind, too, that in situations of abuse, since they are always abuses of power, an apology itself may be viewed with some considerable suspicion by a victim. It is quite likely for a victim to wonder whether an apology is genuine or not, heartfelt from the offender or simply words from them or their lawyers. Is it just a way of seeking closure, for the whole business to go away and not trouble the person any further, a way of dismissing everything?

Where a person comes to the point of making a genuine apology to someone they have harmed by a criminal act, then a consequence of their change of heart and new-found openness and honesty will be the recognition that the police will need to be informed if that has not already happened. If the journey to forgiveness is to be fully received, then it will involve the bringing of light to bear into dark areas as part of the recognition and acceptance of responsibility, but also with the consequence of justice being done and being seen to be done. Truth and transparency require it.

Restitution

The person who genuinely feels remorse will almost certainly want to make amends for their action in whatever way is open to them or helpful. At its most basic, if a person were to steal a small amount of money and subsequently apologize, but with no attempt to repay what was stolen, then, at the very least, their apology would be found wanting. While in cases of theft it may be relatively clear what restitution should entail, in other more complex situations it can be very difficult to know what would or would not be appropriate, but at least exploration of the need can follow.

This is what restorative justice schemes attempt to do. Unlike retributive justice, restorative justice tries to make the justice process more healing for the victim especially, but also for the offender. Recent research analysis has suggested that recidivism rates are lower where restorative justice has been entered into, which may be an indication that it is aiding the healing process for the individuals involved as well as the communities affected by the crime.

Restorative justice schemes have been used, for example, in situations where teenagers daubed graffiti on walls and buildings. They met the owners of the building face to face and heard not only from them as to the harm they had done, but also from members of the public, who had to look at the graffiti, about the effect that the damage had more widely on the neighbourhood. In the light of understanding better the consequences of their actions, the boys wrote apologizing, and were involved in community service helping the professional team that had to remove the graffiti. In a different situation, saving up to contribute to the cost of removing the paint would also have fitted the scheme.

Restorative justice schemes will look for ways in which the offenders can repair physical harm or, if acceptable to the victim, seek to serve them in some other way by fulfilling a task for them or offering a gift of some kind, perhaps of their time or skill, which could be extended to helping other victims of similar crimes. The needs of the community, and the harm done to it, have also to be recognized and so community service of some sort is a common element. Because the offender will meet the victim face to face and see them as a human being, hurt and damaged by their actions, they will be encouraged as well to let the victim know about what they are doing to help repair the harm they have done and thus strengthen their new sense of relating and caring.

Such an approach takes seriously the need for restitution in a way that can help everyone involved. Whether individuals do take part in such a scheme or not, restitution is a vital part of the journey of receiving forgiveness.

Resolve

One of the consequences of this journey of receiving forgiveness will be that it will strengthen the resolve of the offender not to offend again. This requires a person's determination, their commitment and will.

Among the false pictures and caricatures that there can be about the nature of Confession within the Church is the view that it is somehow possible to be forgiven for an act one minute and then go straight out and repeat it. If forgiveness is to be fully received then there must be a resolve not to repeat what has happened, not to fall into the same temptation or commit the same wrong again. Of course, even with the strongest resolve a person can fail. Not one of us can be perfect tomorrow by simply deciding today that we will be, however much we might wish it. Our resolve is necessary along our journey, but not sufficient on its own to achieve our goal. It needs us also to grow in our understanding of what we have done wrong and why, what the trigger points for our actions may have been, and to take steps not just to stop but also to remove the opportunities. We need help from outside ourselves. Alcoholics Anonymous and Gamblers Anonymous know this all too well. Those addicted must take steps not to put themselves into positions where they and others can tell in advance that their resolve, of itself, may be insufficient. They know that they need all the help they can get, which includes circles and groups of support, choosing their friends wisely and assuring that those closest to them are aware of their weaknesses and when especially they might need help and encouragement or indeed to be challenged. Counselling and other agencies may give vital assistance, too, not least in helping them to understand themselves better, together with the risks they face and might pose to others. What is true for addicts of alcohol, drugs or gambling has parallels for us all with our own particular needs and weaknesses.

There is much here that has a profound bearing on our prison system, not least to enable it to be more reforming and to avoid returning prisoners at the end of their sentences to the very communities, relationships and situations most likely to make them reoffend.

The resolve not to repeat what has been done wrong is given a formal structure in relation to those who have been convicted of abuse against children. They are required to have a written and signed Agreement, which will be drawn up to fit their own situation. Above all, it will be designed to help protect children, but also to protect the abuser against themselves.

There are some situations where the resolve of a person not to offend again will need them to break off a relationship or membership of a group completely, because the risks associated with continuing are deemed to be too great. Formal risk assessments can help identify such situations and be a very practical outworking and support for the resolve of the person assessed.

In such situations, reconciliation between the one offended against and the offender will never be possible, and this is likely to be understood mutually. In a corresponding way, there are very many victims and survivors of all manner of trauma and horror who would never want to countenance reconciliation, at least as far as they can tell, because the hurts are too painful and deep. As we have recognized, there are those who do not wish to offer any kind of forgiveness and certainly have no desire for any contact with the one who has hurt them, let alone an ongoing relationship. If that is and remains the case, then reconciliation can never be achieved.

There are others who may be able to forgive but for whom reconciliation would be meaningless because the one who had offended them was a stranger and remains so. In such situations, forgiveness can be both offered and received but without any sustained relationship.

Reconciliation

For those, however, who do want to risk offering forgiveness and walking the journey, reconciliation becomes a possibility if the one who has wronged and harmed them chooses to walk their corresponding journey of receiving forgiveness, with the steps outlined above.

Reconciliation itself can be achieved at varying levels, though at its fullest speaks of that which was damaged or fractured being restored, healed and made one. When William Tyndale was translating the Bible into English in the early sixteenth century, he came across many instances where translating the Hebrew proved immensely problematic because there was no English word or phrase that really corresponded to the necessary meaning. In one case in particular, he decided that the need was so great that the only satisfactory way forward was to create a new word, which is how *atonement* came to be born, literally *at-one-ment*. This speaks of the deepest reconciliation, the fullest way for a relationship to be made whole, restored.

This is the goal and essence of the two journeys of forgiveness, the offering and the receiving, where they embrace. It is how reconciliation is meant to be. Indeed, there are some who will regard reconciliation as something unique, which either is or is not achieved and which cannot, therefore, be qualified or partially exist. From this perspective, the much-acclaimed Truth and Reconciliation Commission in South Africa raises concerns, despite the way in which it has achieved so much success and enabled a nation to move forward after the horrors of apartheid. There may have been no other route which could have enabled the country to take such decisive steps to a new beginning, but for some it will not have made possible the desired-for reconciliation because it did not enable justice to be done and be seen to be done. Speaking, seeing and knowing the truth are crucial steps along the way, but do not themselves bring one to the journey's end while those who have admitted gross inhumanities remain unaccountable to the law. The Good Friday Agreement in Northern Ireland sought a similar way of making political and social progress, and, like the Truth and Reconciliation

Commission, has achieved a vast amount but cannot bring about the deepest reconciliation for the same reason.

In the light of the experiences of South Africa, the people of Rwanda chose to follow a different path, one that was already embedded in their own culture. They established not only the International Tribunal Court for Rwanda but also more than 12,000 Gacaca courts to try an estimated 1.2 million cases. These Gacaca courts were based on the principle that 'revealing is healing'. Originally, Gacaca gatherings were meant to restore order and harmony within communities by acknowledging wrongs and having justice restored to those who were victims. The system went a stage further, therefore, than the Truth and Reconciliation Commission in that the Gacaca courts were empowered to give punishments, though rarely prison sentences and more usually community tasks such as rebuilding victims' homes, working in their fields or serving some other community need. This is much more akin to Western restorative justice and establishes stronger, potentially healing, links between victims and their families and the perpetrators of the violence. While, at their best, what these Gacaca courts achieved came closer to local reconciliation and brought about a huge amount that was positive in the communities, yet, inevitably, establishing so many courts so quickly with so little training meant that the experiences were mixed, the legal representation too often poor or even non-existent, the judgements uneven and the opportunity for corruption difficult to avoid.

The national path to peace in Rwanda was not restricted to the Gacaca courts but also focused heavily on keeping the Tutsi Genocide Memorial Day on 7 April with the seven days following becoming a memorial week.

While South Africa, Northern Ireland and Rwanda have all followed different patterns to try to establish peace, justice and reconciliation following years of bloodshed and violence, they have had some similar goals in view, principally the underlying need for truth and openness, the admission and acknowledgement of guilt and harm done. They have made amazing strides forward in their different ways and different situations and moved communities that have been in conflict closer together. However, despite the vast amount of good that they have achieved, they have raised and will continue to raise major questions and concerns about the place of immunity from prosecution, official pardons, the nature of justice and, therefore, the level of reconciliation achievable.

There are, of course, different models and ways of conducting truth commissions, some of which lead to stronger commitments to reparation than others. Many organizations have made and continue to make studies of the different models and try to assess the peace which they help facilitate. It is perhaps not surprising that lasting peace is likely to be strongest in those places where perpetrators of injustices were called most to account. This has been the basis of the establishing and working of the International Court of Justice, International Criminal Courts and Tribunals at The Hague, and also what lay behind the Nuremberg trials after the Second World War. What might be achievable after one conflict might not be possible or appropriate after another.

Clearly, there is no single way forward even if there are similar issues and questions to be faced. One of these concerns the nature of justice itself and can be posed by asking, 'Whose justice?' Just as history is mostly written by the victors, so the question of 'Whose justice?' may be answered more by one group than another. If there is no acknowledgement that there can be varied answers, from very different perspectives, to the same question, then reconciliation is not likely to be achieved because the recognition of the complexity of views and opinions will be absent. While many will see the IRA as terrorists, others will see them as freedom fighters. And what of the role and work of David Ben-Gurion, the first Prime Minister of Israel, in the years prior to 1948, to the establishing of the State of Israel? Nelson Mandela will be mostly remembered as an extraordinarily charismatic President of South Africa, despite being arrested and imprisoned for conspiring against the state. To what extent had Nelson Mandela been a freedom fighter? When did his commitment to non-violent means of overthrowing the obscenity of apartheid begin? Did he stay true to the commitment or break it? Nelson Mandela achieved so much in his life and has been feted in so many ways, not least being held by many South Africans as the 'Father of the Nation' and receiving the Nobel Peace Prize, yet questions remain which may never completely be resolved but have a bearing upon the issue of justice and whose justice.

There may well be stages in the development and emergence of nations when establishing and valuing peace must take political precedence over everything else, including justice. However, if peace, like reconciliation, is to be lasting and full then it is unlikely to be so unless it is firmly based on as complete a truth and justice as possible. Unresolved, hidden or unacknowledged injustices do not go away but fester like everything else that is unhealthy. Whether the festering will break out to cause new sickness and suffering will vary according to the situation and scale of the infection. The festering can continue for many years, or even generations, and can contribute to the breaking out anew of old conflicts. The wars and fighting in the Balkans and Yemen bear witness to that, as do experiences of conflict in many other parts of the world.

Reconciliation remains the goal. It needs working at by those first affected by the conflicts and tragedies, and also by their children and their children's children.

It is all too clear that the issues facing nations and whole communities carry levels of complexity and interconnectedness which can never fully be unravelled or understood. The principles of the way of offering and receiving forgiveness which are necessary to achieve reconciliation in personal relationships still have their vital importance on the macro scale, where they are so much more difficult to apply. They may need levels of political compromise that do not have to be countenanced on the smaller, personal scale and which always risk more unresolved issues flaring up in the future. The issues caused by conflict and division need to be addressed continually and by each generation.

6

Communities responding to tragedy

Those who work with the United Nations or other international organizations in trying to establish lasting peace and reconciliation will be quick to say how the work must always be local and not imported from outside. Insights are clearly learnt from many situations, but it is vital to avoid giving the impression that there is a reliable formula or route to peace that outsiders can bring in, or suggesting that there is a sure or known way of achieving it. Furthermore, there will always be the recognition that the work is part of the total post-conflict reconstruction, which takes a long time to achieve. What is true for nations is true for smaller communities that have suffered from violence or trauma. Each situation will be distinct, both in the nature of the tragedy that has happened but also regarding the community so traumatized and affected.

We have reflected already[1] upon the difficulty for nations and other organizations in apologizing for atrocities done in their name. Similar issues are involved in both the offering of forgiveness as well the receiving of it. We have recognized, too, how political imperatives and resulting compromise can leave unresolved issues that will continue to fester within communities and so risk contributing to future conflict.

How a community responds to a tragedy that befalls it will in part depend upon whether it existed as a community prior to the tragedy or whether it came into being as a community of victims on account of the tragedy. If it was the former, then whether or not it can respond as a community will depend upon many factors, including: whether it owed its existence to ideological, geographical or social factors; the nature of the relationships of members of the community to one another; its size; what leaders it has and how they came to be leaders, as well as how representative they are; what structures and organization the community has within itself; what resources and strength it has. Aberfan, Hungerford, Enniskillen and Beslan all existed as communities prior to the horrors that they had to face. So, too, in a different way the church in Charleston, South Carolina, was a community that existed as a gathered, faith community bound by common beliefs and known leaders before the fateful shootings. Those caught up in the Lockerbie tragedy involved not only the village but also the relatives of all those on the Pan Am Flight 103. In this latter case, not only were people unknown to one another brought together but also the ultimate responsibility for the bombing has remained shrouded in mystery, making any communal response all the harder and more remote.

When the pastor and eight other members of the Emanuel African Methodist Episcopal Church in Charleston were shot by a young white supremacist at a Wednesday evening Bible study on 17 June 2015, members of two of the families, who had loved ones murdered, expressed forgiveness of the killer when he appeared in court less than 48 hours later. When the Revd Anthony Thompson, whose wife Myra was one of the victims, explained his decision to express forgiveness, he said, 'When I forgave him, my peace began. I'm done with him. He doesn't have control of me.'[2]

Anthony Thompson had spoken after Nadine Collier, whose mother Ethel Lance was also a victim. At the judge's invitation, Nadine had gone to the podium and, when there, found herself saying:

> I forgive you. You took something very precious away from me. I will never get to talk to her again – but I forgive you and have mercy on your soul. You hurt me. You hurt a lot of people. If God forgives you, I forgive you.

She has said more recently that she did not regret what she said that day or want to change it. She believes it is what her mother might have said. However, some of the members of her family feel that because Nadine spoke as she did, the focus has been on her and on her forgiveness, rather than on the needs of the family as a whole, or indeed the reactions or attitudes of others affected.

Within any community or family, individuals are bound to have different reactions and want to say different things, at different stages and in different ways.

While two of the families involved had members who expressed forgiveness, the other seven did not, or at least not at that stage and not publicly. The tensions within the Lance family have been mirrored in the church family. There are some who think that offering forgiveness too soon, as they see it, has meant that other underlying issues, especially the racial motive, have not received the attention that they needed and might otherwise have received, not only from the church itself but also from the wider community, if media attention had not been focused elsewhere.

For every community in grief and shock there is the question about how to reach out to those who are hurting so that, on the one hand, they do not feel left alone and isolated, but on the other hand, do not feel swamped and intruded upon. Trying to assess accurately where the boundary lies between these two extremes in each individual case is almost impossible: some will feel that they are receiving the right support, others will not.

Anthony Thompson, the second person in Charleston to express forgiveness, was invited subsequently to speak at a predominantly white church in a neighbouring area and was amazed to hear a woman publicly apologize for having been racist. Her example led others to do the same and so give encouragement to all the people who wanted to see change. The evil of the massacre was being redeemed.

Emanuel Church in Charleston has found, as all communities do, the importance of anniversaries and marking them in a way that continues to build hope and peace, with many white people coming together with black people to worship and express their unity in defiance of the racist attitudes that led to the murders. At the first anniversary service, the congregation sent a special message to the people of Orlando, Florida, who had witnessed an even worse shooting less than a week before the anniversary service.

Communities which have known terrible trauma are in a unique position to be able to use their own experience to reach out with sympathy, understanding and encouragement to others facing something similar. Doing so not only helps the community approached but also the one recovering because it draws out something positive from the experience of coping with the horror as well as enabling them to say and do something in a united way. It can also help them to see how far they have moved on from the initial horror and shock.

The town of Hungerford in Berkshire discovered this, following the bombing in Oslo and subsequent shootings less than two hours later at the summer camp on the island of Utøya in 2011. They later invited the Norwegian Ambassador to their town and sent back a message to Oslo through him that people and communities can recover. They had sent similar messages after the Dunblane and Lockerbie disasters. Hungerford knew from its own experience that recovery is possible and also that the process is ongoing, even 30 years later. It had experienced mass murder on 19 August 1987 when a lone gunman had randomly killed 16 people and injured a similar number. No one ever discovered a motive, which added an extra dimension to the horror. Among the gunman's victims were his own mother and neighbours.

Following the shootings, the mayor and the vicar became in many ways the voices of the small town where so many people knew one another. Its population was only 5,500. The community wanted life to return to 'normal' as soon as it could and to rebuild what had been damaged, but of course the 'new normal' was bound to be very different from the 'old normal', especially for the families in grief. The town was assisted in its work of rebuilding by the great generosity of so many people across the country. Inevitably, the town was in the media spotlight for the days following the shooting and, even now, reporters will say that it is difficult to find people prepared to be interviewed because they felt a sense of intrusion in the days immediately after the tragedy.

Anniversaries, as they bring back memories, have become highlighted in Hungerford and the community has been able also to express mutual support and solidarity by greater attendance at the usual community events. When a school was threatened with closure, the community worked more strongly together than might previously have been the case. People have spoken of barriers being broken down by the shared experiences of grief, loss and bewilderment. Some will also say that the community has become more vibrant. It would be hard to assess whether there has been forgiveness, but the fruits of new life in the community speak of movement along that road. The town made a conscious decision to refer to the event as the 'Tragedy', and that is the word which appears on the memorial which was subsequently erected. Part of the thinking behind this is that the community does not wish to give any focus to the perpetrator of the shootings and he is not referred to in any way on the memorial.

One of the consequences of the Hungerford tragedy was that Parliament changed the law so as to ban semi-automatic weapons. While this was welcomed across the country, it was also seen and felt as a positive outcome by the people of Hungerford, as something good to have emerged from their tragedy. Seeing changes for the better come about assists the healing process for the community and for the people most involved.

The people of Aberfan in south Wales had a clear cause of the horror that swept over them when a waste tip from a nearby colliery slid down the mountainside on 21 October 1966 and engulfed Pantglas Junior school as well as 19 houses. One hundred and forty-four people were killed, of whom 116 were children. A tribunal set up by the Government in response to the disaster published its findings in less than a year, stating that responsibility and blame rested with the National Coal Board. The Inquiry Team wrote that the disaster could and should have been avoided. While heavy rain was the immediate cause of the tip moving, the underlying reason was that it had been built on top of known springs above the village.

Aberfan was a slightly smaller community than Hungerford. As it first tried to cope with the devastation, the chapels in the village played key roles, and their clergy and people with them. Two of the chapels became temporary mortuaries, another one a rest centre for all the emergency service workers, and a further one a support centre for the people bereaved and shocked. There was a huge outpouring of support, not just from the United Kingdom but internationally. The local people especially had to cope with the anger that was in their grief, with the fact that the NCB had allowed this to happen. This became exacerbated when, later on, money from the Disaster Fund was misdirected to supporting the NCB to remove two other nearby tips.

As with Hungerford, so in Aberfan corporate events played key parts in helping the villagers to rebuild shattered lives in a community that could never be the same again. The vital role and work of the chapels continued as did their music and local choirs. Good communication was essential for people to know what was happening, though the presence of so many from national and international media was intrusive. Anniversaries and the different village events of the year were of great importance in the recovery process, though nothing could take away or stop the ongoing grief and pain. Inevitably, all the families and individuals responded in their own ways and at their own speed. One of the school children who survived, when so many did not, found that it was the fiftieth anniversary which provided the trigger for her to begin to weep and express her grief more outwardly for the first time. Not surprisingly, half the survivors experienced post-traumatic stress disorder, while nightmares and guilt at surviving were present too.

In the face of disasters, it is hard enough for individuals to begin to come to terms with what has happened and start their own journeys of forgiveness. Corporate response is even harder, though some catching of a common mood and aspiration can take place at gatherings on anniversaries and at other key community times if there are sensitive leaders. Meeting or knowing that there are others who have experienced something similar can provide a measure of solidarity and support that assists in the grieving process, though hearing of how others are coping can add to the pressure to 'do better' oneself.

Following the terrible terrorist attack in Beslan in north Ossetia in Russia in September 2004, when more than 1,100 people were taken hostage, of whom 334 were killed, more than half of them children, some of the bereaved parents established a group called the Mothers of Beslan. This was primarily a support and advocacy group, but also had a more political agenda. It wanted answers to questions about why the attack took place and exactly who, in addition to the 30 or so terrorists, was responsible. Beslan is a town of more than 36,000 people and so the formation of a group in response to the horrendous siege might have been able to act as a focus for the town as a whole to come to terms together with what had happened. However, within a year the Mothers of Beslan group had divided, with a splinter group calling itself the Voice of Beslan, seeking a similar but slightly less political role.

Clearly, when organized terrorism, with its own local connections, is the immediate reason for a tragedy, as it was in Beslan, then a political agenda compounds the problems of individuals and communities trying to respond to the tragedy. In such circumstances, divisions may increase, which makes the grieving harder still. The anger, which is for many part of the grieving process, does not make the inter-personal relationships of an action group any easier. Also, if there were underlying tensions between individuals or groups within a community before the tragedy, then it is quite likely that they will surface all the more in the anguish that follows.

The experience of the city of Coventry in November 1940 was very different. During the night of the 14th, more than 500 German bombers were involved in the most devastating attack that there had been on any city up until that time during the Second World War, leaving a third of the city centre destroyed, another third badly damaged and most of the rest affected to some degree. Nearly 600 people were killed.

Among the buildings destroyed by the incendiary bombs was the ancient Cathedral of St Michael. The morning after the air raid, the Provost of the Cathedral, Provost Howard, was out among the ruins and vowed that a new cathedral would be built as a sign of hope, forgiveness and reconciliation. The cathedral stonemason, Jock Forbes, had noticed that two of the huge medieval roof timbers, destroyed in the fire, had landed in the shape of a cross. He set up these two charred pieces of timber in the sanctuary on the rubble, where the altar had been before the bombing, and Provost Howard wrote on the wall behind them, 'Father, forgive'. Shortly after, a local priest, the Revd Arthur Wales, took three of the cut, medieval roof nails and created a cross of nails, which quickly became, and has remained, the distinctive sign of Coventry's ministry of reconciliation.

The Cathedral's refusal to let bitterness and the desire for revenge dominate was an inspiration to the whole city and beyond that to the nation. It has remained an inspiration and has shaped not only the development of the Cathedral and diocese but also the city as a whole, which links internationally with many other cities throughout the world that have also been destroyed in war, such as Dresden, Sarajevo and Hiroshima.

The cathedral took the lead in the Coventry response, and perhaps a communal response to tragedy only really becomes possible if there is clear and inspired leadership to motivate it, with a positive conviction and vision to uphold it. Having prayed and worked for reconciliation and peace from the blitz of 1940, Coventry Cathedral was given a new focus for its prayer by one of its canon's, Joseph Poole, in 1958 when he composed the Litany of Reconciliation. It is framed around what are called the seven deadly sins[3] and is prayed every weekday at noon in the new cathedral, but in the ruins of the old cathedral on Fridays. It is an invitation for us all to reflect that we, not just some convenient 'them', need forgiving by God and before God. Here is the Litany:

All have sinned and fallen short of the glory of God.
The hatred which divides nation from nation, race from race, class from class,
Father forgive.
The covetous desires of people and nations to possess what is not their own,
Father forgive.
The greed which exploits the work of human hands and lays waste the earth,
Father forgive.
Our envy of the welfare and happiness of others,
Father forgive.
Our indifference to the plight of the imprisoned, the homeless, the refugee,
Father forgive.
The lust which dishonours the bodies of men, women and children,
Father forgive.
The pride which leads us to trust in ourselves and not in God,
Father forgive.
Be kind to one another, tender-hearted, forgiving one another, as God in Christ forgave you.[4]

7

God's forgiveness

The example of Coventry Cathedral and diocese in their ministry of reconciliation, and the way that has inspired and influenced not just the whole city of Coventry but also many others across the UK and internationally, highlights both the work that the church can do as well as the difficulty for a community to find a corporate response when it has no similar group or organization to take a lead and help shape the way forward. The need for forgiveness and reconciliation, rather than bitterness, resentment and revenge, is true for all people if they are not to be in the same prison as the Vietnam veteran who was standing in front of the Washington Memorial.[1] Those who have discovered their own journey of forgiveness and begun following it will know the need to be forgiven as well as to forgive. This is true for everyone, and it is the testimony of countless Christians walking this path of forgiveness that it makes most sense when it is understood to be God's own way which we are following. It emanates from God's forgiveness of us, which is part of his unconditional and limitless love.

We are the recipients of that love and forgiveness. We are known, loved, forgiven and free. That is central and formative to everything about us. Our own ability to forgive flows best from this experience of being forgiven, above all by God but also by others. As we have recognized, we pass on what we first receive.

God continually offers us his unconditional love and forgiveness, but we need to be open to it and receive it. As with all forgiveness offered to us, our receiving it is conditional upon our fulfilling the different stages and elements, which we have already considered in Chapter 5. Without that, it remains unconditionally offered forgiveness but unreceived. This is why the good news of the Christian faith has at its core the proclamation of repentance, of turning and beginning again with a change of heart, looking to and following Jesus Christ, receiving his love and forgiveness.

At the end of St Luke's Gospel, the risen Christ gives his disciples their final commission: 'Thus it is written, that the Messiah is to suffer and to rise from the dead on the third day, and that repentance and forgiveness of sins is to be proclaimed in his name to all nations'.[2] Repentance and forgiveness are at the heart of Jesus' own teaching and life. They are his final words to his followers and friends. They were almost his last words in life when he said from the cross, 'Father, forgive them; for they do not know what they are doing.'[3] That was a prayer made while he was still being tortured, but still able to reach out in love as he had done throughout his life. He was putting into practice what he taught about loving our enemies and doing good to those who hate us.[4] The offer of unconditional love is always part of this love of our enemies, love of those who, to some degree or other, have put themselves over against us and wronged us.

It is as though Jesus on the cross absorbs all that is thrown at him and gives back love. The image of a 'divine sponge' soaking up all the hatred and evil captures something of this. Forgiveness for Jesus is not a matter of giving up the desire for revenge, for with him that desire has no place, room or space because he is filled by love. It is as though God is saying to us in Jesus, 'Here is my Son who loves you with my kind of love, totally, completely. In everything that he says and does, he will demonstrate and live that love for you to experience and follow. You can do what you want to him, but you will not be able to stop him loving you. You can ignore him, if you wish, argue with him, reject him, misrepresent him, mock him, deny him, betray him, torture him, even kill him, but you will not be able to stop him loving. You will not be able to kill that love because it is the strongest power in the universe, the power that brought everything into being, so there will be new life, resurrection, love living and going on.' His forgiveness, and acceptance of us as we are, is part of that love.

Jesus was absolutely consistent in what he said and did, in showing and living love with complete integrity and truth throughout his ministry. One of the earliest healing miracles was for the paralyzed man who was carried to him by his friends. They could not bring the bed near to Jesus because of the crowd around him, so they let it down through the roof of the house in which Jesus was teaching. Jesus' first words to the paralyzed man were, 'Friend, your sins are forgiven you.'[5] When the scribes and Pharisees who were present began to question what Jesus had said, he answered them: '"Why do you raise such questions in your hearts? Which is easier, to say, 'Your sins are forgiven you,' or to say, 'Stand up and walk'? But so that you may know that the Son of Man has authority on earth to forgive sins" – he said to the one who was paralyzed – "I say to you, stand up and take your bed and go to your home."'[6] Immediately, the man did just that. Jesus had perceived the reason for the paralysis and knew that just as not offering forgiveness leaves us in prison, so too not receiving forgiveness ultimately leaves us paralyzed, locked up. He saw the issue and acted upon it, releasing and healing the bound man.

Jesus' key teaching about forgiveness comes not only in how he acts but also in the parable which he gives in response to Peter's question as to how many times he should forgive his brother. 'As many as seven times?', asks Peter. Jesus replies, 'Not seven times, but, I tell you, seventy-seven times.'[7] Jesus is not saying count them all up and stop forgiving on the seventy-eighth occasion! He is saying that there is no limit, no counting: forgiveness is to be freely offered because it is freely received. He explains this with the parable about two slaves. The first owes a huge fortune to his master, the king, who is threatening to throw him into prison because he cannot pay. When the man falls on his knees before the king, asking for time to repay, he is forgiven the debt fully. The same slave then comes upon a fellow slave who owes him a much smaller amount. Despite the second slave falling on his knees and asking for time to repay, he is thrown into prison. The fellow slaves are very distressed by what has happened and report it to the king who summons the first slave and says to him, 'You wicked slave! I forgave you all that debt because you pleaded with me. Should you not have had mercy on your fellow-slave, as I had mercy on you?'[8]

The messages are simple and profound. The scale of what we owe and have been forgiven is vastly more than what is owed to us. We are to show mercy and forgive others because we have been shown mercy and forgiveness.

If we grasp the full import of the first of these two truths, then the second follows all the more clearly. But for us to understand how much we have been forgiven we need to see ourselves as we really are, as God sees us, not just as we imagine ourselves to be or want to be. We are back to the issue of 'recognition' that we were considering earlier in Chapter 5.

As St Paul puts it, 'All have sinned and fall short of the glory of God.'[9] The word used by Paul here for sin is taken from the world of archery. It is about missing the mark. The mark is the glory of God, Jesus himself. We do not show the fullness of love and service as Jesus did. We fail to live his love and glory, to be Christ-like, both in what we do and in what we fail to do.

As we have seen earlier, if we are to receive forgiveness we must begin by recognizing and taking responsibility in the right way for who we are and what we have done or failed to do that is less than loving. This is expressed very clearly in the first epistle of St John: 'If we say that we have no sin, we deceive ourselves, and the truth is not in us. If we confess our sins, he who is faithful and just will forgive us our sins and cleanse us from all unrighteousness.'[10]

The ability to justify ourselves in our own eyes is a skill that many of us possess in abundance, which makes it all the harder to recognize and understand the extent to which even the little issues contribute significantly to our missing the mark. As Jesus said in the Sermon on the Mount,[11] it is not just extreme acts such as murder or adultery that are against the commandments but also the inner disposition which can lead to those evils, the inner thoughts motivated by anger and lust.

The call to Christ-likeness is a call to his way of thinking as well as his way of acting. It is a call to purity of heart where all that is against his way of love is squeezed out because there is space only for love. 'It is no longer I who live, but it is Christ who lives in me,'[12] was how St Paul put it. It can be hard for us to recognize that our innermost thoughts contribute to the store of what is wrong, because it is our thoughts which lead to our actions.

All that is against the way of love adds to the pains and hurts that there are in others and in the heart of God himself. The cross of Christ is the culmination of those pains and hurts, with little actions as well as larger ones all contributing and playing their part. It is for this reason that we need to ask for and receive God's forgiveness.

As the good news of being accepted and forgiven soaks into us, the experience is one of joy and thankfulness. Jesus makes this very clear in the story of the two sons. It is commonly called the story of the prodigal son, but it is in fact about his older brother as well. The younger of the two brothers asks his father for his inheritance to be given to him. When this happens, he leaves home for a distant land and squanders all that he has. He eventually ends up doing the most menial of tasks, feeding pigs, because he is in need and there is a famine in the land.

When he came to himself he said, 'How many of my father's hired hands have bread enough and to spare, but here I am dying of hunger! I will get up and go to my father, and I will say to him, "Father, I have sinned against heaven and before you; I am no longer worthy to be called your son; treat me like one of your hired hands."' So he set off and went to his father. But while he was still far off, his father saw him and had compassion; he ran and put his arms around him and kissed him. Then the son said to him, 'Father, I have sinned against heaven and before you; I am no longer worthy to be called your son.' But the father said to his slaves, 'Quickly, bring out a robe – the best one – and put it on him; put a ring on his finger and sandals on his feet. And get the fatted calf and kill it, and let us eat and celebrate; for this son of mine was dead and is alive again; he was lost and is found!' And they began to celebrate.[13]

The older brother was angry when he heard the music and discovered the reason for it and refused to join the celebration. His father came out to plead with him, but the truth was that he saw himself not as a son but as a slave, working for his father without joy. His was a world where duty squeezed out joy rather than lived happily with it.

Receiving the unconditional forgiveness as a son or daughter, being alive rather than dead, found rather than lost, is cause for celebration, joy and thanksgiving. That is the empowering truth of the gospel and of life. It enables life to be lived in all its fullness, not because we then wantonly miss the mark again, relying on being forgiven once more, but rather because the experience of life in its fullness changes us and makes us want to aim for the mark, aim for the glory of God, for Jesus' quality of living, for being the best we can be. We aim with the renewed energy and delight given by God himself. Of course, we still miss the mark, still come up short and need forgiving, but we know where we belong, with whom we belong; we know where home is, where we are loved and accepted as we are. We are empowered to try again, to be changed and to flourish.

The younger brother in Jesus' story had tried to live joy without duty. The older brother lived duty without joy. Duty and joy need one another, they belong together, and, as we say in our Holy Communion week by week, 'It is our duty and our joy at all times and in all places to give [God] thanks and praise.'

In order to drive home this message of the joy of forgiveness, the story of the lost or prodigal son is preceded in St Luke's Gospel by two other stories of joy at the lost being found. First, there is the story of the lost sheep. 'Rejoice with me, for I have found my sheep that was lost,' says the shepherd. Then, immediately after, there is the story of the woman who lost a coin which she then finds after searching carefully everywhere. She calls together her friends and neighbours, 'Rejoice with me, for I have found the coin that I had lost.'[14] So strong is this theme of the joy and grace of forgiveness that St Paul even asks, 'Should we continue in sin in order that grace may abound? By no means! How can we who died to sin go on living in it?'[15]

The woman taken in adultery discovered the joy of being forgiven when Jesus protected her from being stoned to death and forgave her.[16] Zacchaeus unexpectedly found the healing, forgiving and transforming effect of the presence and generous love of Jesus and responded with newly empowered generosity of his own.[17] Peter experienced this as well on the lakeshore after the resurrection, when Jesus invited him to profess his love three times, just as he had only those few days earlier three times denied even knowing Jesus.[18] Jesus returning to the disciples after his resurrection was an expression of love and forgiveness for all of them, for each had deserted him and fled, but he came back, accepting, forgiving, affirming, valuing, commissioning, loving. The penitent thief on the cross had experienced that wonder when Jesus said to him, 'Truly, I tell you, today you will be with me in Paradise.'[19]

A friend of mine once expressed the view that Jesus forgiving the penitent thief on the cross gave him an excuse to ignore the whole gospel: he would live his life entirely as he chose, as self-indulgently or selfishly as he wanted, he said, and then, on his deathbed, repent and all would be made well. Quite apart from the serious issue that he might have a sudden death, this plan totally misunderstands the nature of repentance and forgiveness, that they are journeys. If we are given a choice to walk a path and decline to take it once, then perhaps other opportunities will come again. If we repeatedly refuse to take the offered path, then we risk losing the ability to say 'Yes' because we have so practised the habit of saying 'No'. Any habit is formative and shapes our development, which is why it is so much better if we can learn the path of forgiveness when young. We are shaped by forgiving just as we are shaped by not forgiving, which hardens our hearts. There is a journey of not forgiving, just as there is a journey of forgiving.

Jesus said that all things could be forgiven except the sin against the Holy Spirit.[20] This is surely because to sin against the Holy Spirit is to call goodness evil, truth a lie, darkness light, love hate. In a state of such complete reversal and denial, forgiveness simply cannot be received, the journey cannot be taken, the road is barred, light and love no longer have a way in. This is where continued rejection of the offer of God's love can lead if we become totally shaped and frozen by it. If anyone is anxious lest they have committed such a sin, then their very anxiety shows that they have not. God, who knows all the secrets of our hearts, knows also how to offer us repeatedly the invitation to turn and follow him.

It is because we experience the free gift of God's forgiveness that we are also empowered to forgive ourselves. Because God loves us, we are given life and worth. We are called to love what God loves, and God loves us. If God values us as human beings, made in his image, how can we not value all other people and ourselves with them? Not to value ourselves is to deny God's creation and loving presence in us. It is to say that God has got it wrong, made a mistake, and that it is OK for him to love all those other people, but not us. If only he knew us better, he would realize that we are not lovable at all.

Learning to see and value ourselves in the way that God does is the way of humility. Pride, its opposite, sees things its own way rather than God's way. Pride wants us to put ourselves, rather than God, at the centre of everything. The first of the two creation stories in the book of Genesis has God making humankind in his own image.[21] Pride makes us try to retaliate by usurping the place of God and attempting to make God in our image, the way we want him to be.

Jesus told the parable of the Pharisee and the publican or tax collector, to drive home this point about the opposite responses of pride and humility. Not only is it the case that we can only receive God's love and forgiveness in a spirit of humility, it is pride which leads to a distorted false love of self.

> Two men went up to the temple to pray, one a Pharisee and the other a tax collector. The Pharisee, standing by himself, was praying thus, 'God, I thank you that I am not like other people: thieves, rogues, adulterers, or even like this tax collector. I fast twice a week; I give a tenth of all my income.' But the tax collector, standing far off, would not even look up to heaven, but was beating his breast saying, 'God, be merciful to me, a sinner!' I tell you, this man went down to his home justified rather than the other; for all who exalt themselves will be humbled, but all who humble themselves will be exalted.[22]

There is a right kind of love of self as well as wrong kinds. Self-esteem and self-respect express the proper kind of self-love and are over against the puffed-up, exaggerated distortion of love that comes from pride on the one hand and from the self-hating rejection of self on the other. These alternative paths lead to a lack of forgiving ourselves, because both lead to a lack of loving ourselves. Both lead to our inability to receive God's love and forgiveness.

Self-forgiveness starts with self-acceptance and humility, which enable us to see ourselves as we really are, as God sees us and knows us to be. Self-forgiveness builds our self-esteem because it expresses our proper love of self, 'warts and all'. Its journey involves our understanding ourselves more and more fully and so accepting ourselves at an ever-deeper level. We find that we can love ourselves, despite the hidden, darkest, meanest, least likeable parts of ourselves, knowing that God sees all these and still loves us, giving us the confidence to risk loving ourselves. If God can love 'me', then surely that must mean that there is something lovable in me and I can learn to love 'me' too. Loving is not the same as liking, and just as we can love other people while not necessarily liking every bit of them, so the same is true for ourselves.

It is those who know themselves to be loved and forgiven who are most able to live freely, to grow, develop and risk newness openly. When Jesus came to Jericho on his way up to Jerusalem, he met a blind man called Bartimaeus. Jesus asked him, 'What do you want me to do for you?'[23] This may seem a rather strange question when it was obvious that the man was blind and being healed would change everything. In that sense, it was inescapably a risk, unknown in so many respects. Healing would take Bartimaeus on a completely new path. Is this what he really wanted? It was, but he had to say so, he had to choose it, for Jesus would never impose or take away his free will, or ours. Bartimaeus was given his sight. The first person he saw would have been Jesus, and he followed him as a disciple.

Just as healing and forgiveness let us see fully and clearly, so we need to be open to the gift. This was expressed very forcibly by Jesus in his earlier miracle of healing a deaf mute. Jesus said to him, 'Ephphatha', that is, 'Be opened'.[24] As so often with the Gospels, a word or saying deliberately has a wider meaning and significance than that in its own specific context. Unless we live in that openness to God all the time, then we shall not be able to hear or see the things of deepest and most profound importance. Ephphatha was such a key word for St Mark that he kept the Aramaic original that Jesus would have spoken in order to emphasize its significance.

When Lazarus was raised from the dead and came out of the tomb, Jesus said, 'Unbind him, and let him go.'[25] These words also resonate elsewhere. God's love and forgiveness unbind and free us from all that restricts us, all that stops us growing and flourishing. We are people who are forgiven, who are loved and freed from all that would hold us back, including all our past mistakes, but also the unrelenting demands of perfectionism on the one hand and fear of failure on the other.

Our response to this overwhelming sense of being set free and forgiven is one of joy and thankfulness. That was Christian's experience in John Bunyan's *Pilgrim's Progress* when his burden fell away at the cross and he knew himself loved and forgiven.

It must also have been the experience of Onesimus about whom St Paul wrote to Philemon in the epistle that bears his name. Onesimus was Philemon's slave but found himself in Rome where he was converted through Paul's ministry. Paul wanted Onesimus to return to Philemon and sent the letter with him, asking Philemon to accept him back as a brother and forgive him for whatever it was that he had done to wrong Philemon. 'If you consider me your partner,' Paul wrote, 'welcome him as you would welcome me. If he has wronged you in any way, or owes you anything, charge that to my account. I, Paul, am writing this with my own hand: I will repay it.'[26] We do not know the outcome of this appeal but can only assume that Philemon will have forgiven Onesimus and maybe given him his freedom, so that he could indeed return to Paul as a brother and continue to work with him while he was in prison in Rome. What is intriguing here, among other things, is that Paul is reminding Philemon how much he, Philemon, owes Paul and that, if there is any reluctance on his part to forgive Onesimus, then he should do so because of that debt to Paul.

We have seen the link between debt and forgiveness a number of times already and it is there many times in the Gospels and Epistles. Indeed, it is possible that the root meaning of the word *guilt* comes to us originally from the German word for money, *geld*. If so, then it is a further link between the language of forgiving debts and forgiving offences.

It was money that the two owed in the parable that Jesus told in Matthew 18, and it was of course money that was involved with the story of the two debtors that Jesus told when he was in the house of Simon the Pharisee. One of the two owed ten times the amount that the other owed. Both had their debts cancelled. 'Which of them will love him (the creditor) more?', asked Jesus.

Simon answered, 'I suppose the one for whom he cancelled the greater debt.' And Jesus said to him, 'You have judged rightly.' Then turning towards the woman, he said to Simon, 'Do you see this woman? I entered your house; you gave me no water for my feet, but she has bathed my feet with her tears and dried them with her hair. You gave me no kiss, but from the time I came in she has not stopped kissing my feet. You did not anoint my head with oil, but she has anointed my feet with ointment. Therefore, I tell you, her sins, which were many, have been forgiven; hence she has shown great love.'[27]

It is the same theme which is there in the Lord's Prayer. Our Father in heaven forgives us our trespasses/debts, many though they are, and we in our turn are to forgive others.[28] If we do not, then it calls into question whether we have grasped the significance of being forgiven ourselves, whether we have truly welcomed and accepted the forgiveness offered us. Without that acceptance, that receiving, we are unable to be fully forgiven.

Fully grasping the significance of being forgiven is not something that comes about through our intellectual study or even just reading a book! Forgiveness certainly involves our wills, minds and understanding, but it also involves our 'hearts'. Jesus gave a warning 'to every one of you if you do not forgive your brother or sister from your heart'.[29] The 'heart' was not just the focus for emotions and feelings, but rather the integrated centre of one's being where thought, feeling and belief were to come together in a united way. The heart referred to the depth of our being; it was bound up with what today we would speak of in terms of our integrity, our personality, our character, our essence. Offering and receiving forgiveness were, in other words, far from superficial, certainly not just a matter of a right formula or right words, not something to touch only a part of who we are. Rather, they are to touch and come from the depths of our being.

The Bible often uses this language of the heart. We are to love God with all our heart. The pure in heart are blessed. It is also from the heart that good and evil thoughts come. We have to beware not to harden our hearts. You are to write God's words and teaching 'on the tablet of your heart'.[30]

Forgiveness is to be profound, heart-felt but also heart-located.

It is because forgiveness is so central to the gospel and central to the meaning of Jesus' death on the cross that the Church has the sacrament of penance, as it is known by some, or sacramental confession: the possibility for any person to confess their sins and faults before God, in the presence of a priest, and receive the assurance of sins forgiven in the words of absolution pronounced aloud. The forgiveness received in this way is no different from the forgiveness received by a person privately and quietly confessing their sins and faults to God anywhere and at any time. We all have that direct access to God in prayer. For some, it can be problematic at times to believe and accept that they are indeed forgiven. Hearing a priest pronounce God's forgiveness can enable that reality to touch our ears, minds and hearts more deeply. This can be of particular importance if we have difficulty forgiving ourselves.

A priest is only able to proclaim forgiveness in God's name after the person confessing their sins has done so in a way that acknowledges the different elements that we have already considered in Chapter 5. Without those elements being present, absolution can, and in some cases should, be withheld. This would happen in an extreme situation, for example if someone was confessing some terrible act that was also a crime but, on questioning by the priest, made it clear that they had not been to the police or sought in any way to make amends of any kind. In such a situation, the priest would not only withhold pronouncing absolution but also urge the penitent to go to the police, and indeed do so themselves if the matter was spoken about other than within the 'seal of the confessional' and involved the disclosure of a serious crime such as child abuse or murder.

The epistle of James has an important passage that links forgiveness to healing but also to the ministry of the 'elders of the church' and so to the practice of sacramental confession.

> Are any among you sick? They should call for the elders of the church and have them pray over them, anointing them with oil in the name of the Lord. The prayer of faith will save the sick, and the Lord will raise them up; and anyone who has committed sins will be forgiven. Therefore confess your sins to one another, and pray for one another, so that you may be healed.[31]

This passage also takes us back to the vital theme that unforgiveness damages our health and well-being because of the intimate relationship of body, mind and spirit. The health of each part of us has consequences for the other parts and affects the whole. Physical well-being is not divorced from spiritual or mental well-being.

The call to live as forgiven individuals and as a forgiven community is the call of all people and of the whole Church. St Paul puts this emphatically and clearly when he writes to the Christians in Colossae:

> As God's chosen ones, holy and beloved, clothe yourselves with compassion, kindness, humility, meekness, and patience. Bear with one another and, if anyone has a complaint against another, forgive each other; just as the Lord has forgiven you, so you also must forgive. Above all, clothe yourselves with love, which binds everything together in perfect harmony.[32]

This same central theme of our calling to live love and forgiveness in unity and perfect harmony as people who are loved and forgiven is expressed by St Paul to the Christians in Corinth:

> If anyone is in Christ, there is a new creation; everything old has passed away; see, everything has become new! All this is from God, who reconciled us to himself through Christ, and has given us the ministry of reconciliation; that is, in Christ God was reconciling the world to himself, not counting their trespasses against them, and entrusting the message of reconciliation to us. So we are ambassadors for Christ, since God is making his appeal through us; we entreat you on behalf of Christ, be reconciled to God.[33]

The work of reconciliation is fundamental to the life of Christians and the Church because it was fundamental to Jesus' own life and ministry. It is about being one with God and with one another, removing all the obstacles in the way: the pains, the hurts, damage, self-interests, conflicts, anger, bitterness, everything that stops or fights against unity and peace.

We have discovered consistently that identifying and removing these barriers is costly. It cost Jesus his life on the cross because he insisted on living vulnerable, open, unconditional love in the face of everything. He did this in a unique way, never before seen or known. Everything about him was loving. His total living of love broke down the walls of division and began a new path where new beginnings were possible because forgiveness was possible, and in every situation. This is why St Paul speaks of there now being a 'new creation'.[34] A new path has been begun, a new way of living our humanity. We no longer have to be held back by guilt and everything that is wrong in our own or other people's lives. We are free to live, free to love, free to be more like Jesus himself, free to live God's way. It is the way that can be trusted as a path for all to experience and follow because Jesus has opened it up and walked it himself. It can be received and then offered and passed on. Jesus started a chain reaction. Love and forgiveness are catching. They spread as the good news of the gospel spreads. The first Christians lived an infectious simplicity and harmony of life, reconciled to God and one another, holding all things in common, sharing their resources along with everything else.

The reconciled life is one that is possible because of Christ's life, death and resurrection, but it needs each of us to receive the offered gift and walk the path of forgiveness, both as ones who receive forgiveness but also as ones who offer it when we ourselves are wronged. Reconciliation, as we have reflected, is at the end of those paths when both parties join in the way of forgiveness. This is what God initiates again and again. This is his desire, for us all to receive his love and forgiveness and let the barriers that we have put up be taken down permanently. He longs for us to receive his gift and then use it, to join the ranks of those who live reconciliation and work for it in every situation and relationship.

We are to embody forgiveness and reconciliation, both as individuals and corporately, because we are already loved, accepted and forgiven. This truth is to touch the very depths of our being. This is our life. This is our calling, to be reconciled in harmony, peace, unity and love with God and with one another, receiving the forgiveness bestowed on us and passing it on, offering our own forgiveness to others as we learn more and more to love unconditionally, just as we are loved in this way by God. This is the way for all of us. This is our freedom. This is the gift to us. This is our hope. This is our journey.

Notes

Scripture quotations are from the New Revised Standard Version of the Bible, copyright 1989 by the Division of Christian Education on the National Council of the Churches of Christ in the USA. Used by permission. All rights reserved.

1 *Why forgiveness matters*

1 Winter 1999.
2 Dietrich Bonhoeffer, *The Cost of Discipleship*, London: SCM Press, 1959, p. 35ff.
3 Developed by John J. Sherwood and John C. Glidewell, 'Planned Renegotiations: A Norm-Setting OD Intervention', in *The 1973 Annual Handbook for Group Facilitators*, Iowa City, IA: University Associates, 1973, pp. 195–202. Extended by John J. Sherwood and John J. Scherer, 'A Model for Couples: How Two Can Grow Together', *Small Group Behaviour* 6:1 (February 1975), pp. 11–29.

2 *What is forgiveness?*

1 Ps. 55.12–14; cf. Ps. 41.9.
2 Deborah van Deusen Hunsinger, in Alistair McFadyen and Marcel Sarot (eds), *Forgiveness and Truth*, London: Bloomsbury, 2001, p. 96.
3 John Monbourquette, *How to Forgive*, Ottawa: Novalis, 2000, p. 46.
4 *The Anchor Yale Bible Dictionary*, New York: Doubleday, 1992, p. 831.

3 *Who can forgive?*

1 Lucy Faithfull Foundation website: www.lucyfaithfull.org.uk.
2 Dietrich Bonhoeffer, *The Cost of Discipleship*, London: SCM Press, 1959, p. 36.
3 Bonhoeffer, *Cost*, pp. 40, 42.
4 See, for example, *The Oxford Mail*, 21 December 2017.

5 Matt. 5.48.

6 1 Cor. 13.5 (NEB).

4 Offering forgiveness

1 See, for example, Dr Elisabeth Kubler-Ross's five stages of grief.

2 Terry Waite, interviewed by Heather Bellamy, *Cross Rhythms*, 1 August 2017.

3 Lesley Bilinda, *The Colour of Darkness*, London: Hodder and Stoughton, 1996; *With What Remains*, London: Hodder and Stoughton, 2006.

4 Bilinda, *With What Remains*, p. 200.

5 Lesley Bilinda, 'Remembering Well: The Role of Forgiveness in Remembrance', *Anvil* 30:2 (September 2014).

6 Desmond M. Tutu and Mpho A. Tutu, *The Book of Forgiving*, London: William Collins, 2014.

7 John Monbourquette, *How to Forgive,* Ottawa: Novalis, 2000.

8 Ezek. 36.26; cf. Ezek. 11.19.

9 House of Bishops of the Church of England, *Responding Well to Those who have been Sexually Abused*, London: Church House Publishing, 2011, p. 11.

10 Antoine Leiris, *You Will Not Have My Hate,* London: Harvill Secker, 2016, p. 54.

11 Marie M. Fortune, 'Forgiveness: The Last Step', in Carol J. Adams and Marie M. Fortune (eds), *Violence against Women and Children: A Christian Theological Sourcebook,* New York: Continuum, 1995.

12 David Kerr interviewed by Helen Weathers for the *Daily Mail*, 6 January 2017

13 Corrie ten Boom, with John and Elizabeth Sherrill, *The Hiding Place*, London: Hodder and Stoughton, 2004, pp. 164–5.

14 Ten Boom, *The Hiding Place*, p. 219.

15 Ten Boom, *The Hiding Place*, pp. 220–1.

16 See *The Lambeth Daily*, issue 15, 7 August 1998 (The Official Newspaper of the Lambeth Conference), available online at: http://justus. anglican.org/resources/Lambeth1998/Lambeth-Daily/07/fatherwitness. html.

17 Eric Lomax, *The Railway Man*, London: Vintage, 1996, pp. 240, 241.

18 Lomax, *The Railway Man*, p. 210.

19 Lomax, *The Railway Man*, p. 242.

20 Lomax, *The Railway Man*, pp. 252, 253.

21 Lomax, *The Railway Man*, p. 255.

22 Ex. 21.24.

23 Lomax, *The Railway Man*, p. 206.

24 Kristin Jacks, on the website www.servantsasia.org.

25 Eric Segal, *Love Story*, London: Hodder and Stoughton, 1970.

26 *The Guardian*, 27 April 2017.

27 *Arkansas Times*, 28 April 2017.

5 Receiving forgiveness

1 2 Sam. 11—12.

2 Matt. 13.1–23.

3 Luke 15.11–32.

4 Luke 10.25–37.

5 Matt. 25.31–46.

6 Gen. 3.10.

7 For example, John 3.19–20.

8 On cycles of abuse, see, for example, Lucy Faithfull Foundation, including their *Stop It Now!* programme

9 Ex. 20.5.

6 Communities responding to tragedy

1 See pp. 34–41 above.

2 *Time Magazine*, Charleston shooting cover story. A special report on the June 2015 Charleston shooting.

3 The seven deadly sins are pride, envy, covetousness, lust, anger, gluttony and sloth.

4 Reproduced courtesy of Coventry Cathedral.

7 God's forgiveness

1 See p. 1 above.

2 Luke 24.46–47.

3 Luke 23.34.

4 Luke 6.27.

5 Luke 5.20.

6 Luke 5.22–24.

7 Matt. 18.21–22.

8 Matt. 18.33.

9 Rom. 3.23.

10 1 John 1.8–9.

11 Matt. 5.1—7.27.

12 Gal. 2.20.

13 Luke 15.17–24.

14 Luke 15.6, 9.

15 Rom. 6.1–2.

16 John 8.2–11.
17 Luke 19.1–10.
18 John 21.15–17.
19 Luke 23.43.
20 Mark 3.28–29.
21 Gen. 1.26.
22 Luke 18.10–14.
23 Mark 10.51.
24 Mark 7.34.
25 John 11.44.
26 Philemon 17–19.
27 Luke 7.42–47.
28 Matt. 6.12; Luke 11.4.
29 Matt. 18.35.
30 Mark 12.30; Matt. 5.8; Matt. 12.35; Matt. 15.19; Ps. 95.8; Prov. 3.3 and 7.3.
31 James 5.14–16.
32 Col. 3.12–14.
33 2 Cor. 5.17–20.
34 2 Cor. 5.17; Gal. 6.15.

References and further reading

Adams, Carol J. and Fortune, Marie M. (eds), 1995, *Violence against Women and Children: A Christian Theological Sourcebook*, New York: Continuum.

The Anchor Yale Bible Dictionary, 1992, New York: Doubleday.

Arnold, Johann Christoph, 1998, *The Lost Art of Forgiving*, Robertsbridge, Sussex: Plough Publishing House.

Bash, Anthony, 2011, *Just Forgiveness*, London: SPCK.

Bilinda, Lesley, 1996, *The Colour of Darkness*, London: Hodder and Stoughton.

Bilinda, Lesley, 2006, *With What Remains*, London: Hodder and Stoughton.

Bonhoeffer, Dietrich, 1959, *The Cost of Discipleship*, trans. R. H. Fuller, 6th (complete) edn, London: SCM Press.

Bunyan, John, 2013, *The Pilgrim's Progress*, London: William Collins.

Frankl, Viktor E., 2011, *Man's Search for Meaning*, London: Ebury Publishing.

Frayling, Nicholas, 1996, *Pardon and Peace*, London: SPCK.

Holloway, Richard, 2002, *On Forgiveness*, Edinburgh: Canongate Books.

House of Bishops of the Church of England, 2011, *Responding Well to Those who have been Sexually Abused*, London: Church House Publishing.

Hugo, Victor, 2012, *Les Misérables*, trans. Norman Denny, London: Penguin Books.

Jones, Gregory, 1995, *Embodying Forgiveness*, Grand Rapids, MI: Eerdmans.

Kübler-Ross, Elisabeth, 1969, *On Death and Dying*, London: Routledge.

Leiris, Antoine, 2016, *You Will Not Have My Hate*, London: Harvill Secker.

Lomax, Eric, 1996, *The Railway Man*, London: Vintage.

McFadyen, Alistair and Sarot, Marcel (eds), 2001, *Forgiveness and Truth*, London: Bloomsbury.

Moberly, R. C., *Atonement and Personality*, 1901, London: John Murray.

Monbourquette, John, 2000, *How to Forgive*, Ottawa: Novalis.

Nouwen, Henri, 1994, *The Wounded Healer*, London: Darton, Longman and Todd.

Parker, Russ, 1993, *Forgiveness is Healing*, London: Darton, Longman and Todd.

Parker, Russ, 1988, *Healing Dreams*, London: Triangle, SPCK.

Rose, Gillian, 1995, *Love's Work*, London: Chatto and Windus.

Saward, Jill, with Green, Wendy, 1990, *Rape: My Story*, London: Bloomsbury.

Selby, Peter, 1997, *Grace and Mortgage*, London: Darton, Longman and Todd.

Syed, Matthew, 2015, *Black Box Thinking*, London: Hodder and Stoughton.

Sykes, Stephen, 1997, *The Story of Atonement*, London: Darton, Longman and Todd.

Ten Boom, Corrie, with John and Elizabeth Sherrill, 2004, *The Hiding Place*, London: Hodder and Stoughton.

Tutu, Desmond, 1999, *No Future without Forgiveness*, London: Rider.

Tutu, Desmond M. and Tutu, Mpho A., 2014, *The Book of Forgiving*, London: William Collins.

Volf, Miroslav, 1996, *Exclusion and Embrace*, Nashville, TN: Abingdon Press.

Waite, Terry, 2016, *Taken on Trust*, London: Hodder and Stoughton.

Wiesenthal, Simon, 1970, *The Sunflower*, Paris: Opera Mundi.

Wiesenthal, Simon, 1997, *The Sunflower: On the Possibilities and Limits of Forgiveness*, 2nd rev. edn, New York: Schocken Books.

Wilson, Gordon, with Alf McCreary, 1990, *Marie*, London: Marshall Pickering.

Index of Names and Subjects